LA VACA
Punta del Camello
Bañaderos
San Andrés
Cambalud
Arucas
Firgas
El Toscon
El Palmar
Monte Lentiscal
Punta Casa Blanca
Tafira Baja
Tafira Alta
PLAYA DE LA LAJA
Punta del Palo
Teror
Valleseco
Sgdo. Corazón
Mazagán
Jinamar
Santa Brgídia
La Atalaya
La Gran Parada
Valle de San Roque
Telde
La Estrella
PLAYA D. LA GARITA
Ariñez
San Mateo
Telde
La Garita
Las Lagunetas
Valsequillo de G.C.
ElCaracol
Melenara
Rincón
La Colomba
Playa de Salinetas
Punta de Silva
La Breña
B. de Silva
Cuevas Blancas
Pasadilla
Ruinas Históricas
Rico Blanco
Arguatona
Punta de Gando
Museo
San Bartolome de Tirajana
Ingenio
Aeropuerto de Gando
Carrizal
Santa Lucia
Temisas
Agüimes
Teheral
912
PLAYA DEL BURRERO
Presa de Tirajana
Fataga
Presa de Fataga
B. de la Angostura
Mñ. de Arinaga
198
Punta de la Sal
Puercos
1001
El Estanco
Barranco de Tirajana
Arinaga
Punta del Mato
Cruce de Sardina
Sardina
B. de Fataga
Bahia de Arinaga
Aldea Blanca
Los Blancos
Vecindario
Canón del Aguila
Juan Grande
Punta de Tenefe
La Caleta
El Matorral
Barco Quebrado
Atlantic Ocean
PLAYA DEL CARDÓN
San Agustin
Berriel
PLAYA DE TARAJALILLO
PLAYA DEL INGLÉS
Punta de Maspalomas

The Canary Islands
120 km / 75 miles
Atlantic Ocean
Atlantic Ocean
Pontevedra
Ponferrada
Valladolid
Zamora
Porto
Duoro
Vila Nova de Gaia
Salamanca
Avila
Covilhã
Talavera de la Reina
Punta Monego
Coimbra
Emb.de Alcantara
SPAIN
Caceres
Punta Carvoeiro
PORTUGAL
Mérida
Lisbon
Don Benito
Badajoz
Almada
Alcácer do Sul
Punta Espichel
Córdoba
Galaroza
Punta de Sines
Beja
Odemira
Seville
ALGARVE
Huelva
Ajamonte
Jerez de la Frontera
Punta de São Vicente
Sagres
Faro
GULF OF CÁDIZ
Cádiz
Gibralta
Strait of Gibraltar
Tangier
Tétouan
Larache
Salé
Kenitra
Fez
Rabat
Meknès
Casablanca
Dar- el- Beida
El- Jadida (Mazagan)
Settat
Quedzem
Benimellal
PORTO SANTO
MADEIRA
Safi
MOROCCO
Essaouira
Marrakesh
Jebel Toubkal 4165
ATLAS
Zagora
Taroudant
Agadir
Bouizakarn
Cap Dráa
LANZAROTE
FUERTEVENTURA
LA PALMA
TENERIFE
Santa Cruz de Tenerife
Tantan
ALGERIA
Tindouf
Cap Juby
Tarfaya
GOMERA
Las Palmas de G.Canaria
GRAN CANARIA
HIERRO
El Aaiún
WESTERN SAHARA
MAURITANIA

INSIGHT POCKET GUIDES

Gran Canaria

Written and Presented by **Margaret Hart**

Margaret Hart

INSIGHT POCKET GUIDES

Insight Pocket Guide:

GRAN CANARIA

Directed by
Hans Höfer

Managing Editor
Andrew Eames

Photography by
Paul Young and others

Design Concept by
V. Barl

Design by
Carlotta Junger

Printed in Singapore by
Höfer Press (Pte) Ltd
Fax: 65-8616438

Distributed in the UK & Ireland by
GeoCenter International UK Ltd
The Viables Center, Harrow Way
Basingstoke, Hampshire RG22 4BJ
ISBN: 9-62421-566-9

Worldwide distribution enquiries:
Höfer Communications Pte Ltd
38 Joo Koon Road
Singapore 2262
ISBN: 9-62421-566-9

Bienvenido

Welcome! Most Europeans know of Gran Canaria, but my aim in these pages is to reveal the less publicised attractions of the island – the delightful fishing villages, the empty coves, the pine-topped mountains – which I have discovered during 11 years of earning a living here as an interpreter and lecturer in tourism. It is this face of Gran Canaria that even committed sunseekers come to admire most – if only they are introduced.

Known by the ancient Greeks as the *makaron nesoi* (Fortunate Islands) and by the Romans as the Land of Eternal Spring, the Canary Islands have always seemed to exist more in myth than in reality. Though Spanish, they lie 100km (62 miles) adrift from the coast of Africa, some 1,000km (620 miles) from Spain, Even mainland Spaniards are hazy on questions about where the archipelago exactly is and what its different islands are like. Most people are surprised by the diversity of Gran Canaria. While people bask in the sun at Playa del Inglés, for example, snow can cap the peaks at Tejeda 40km (25 miles) inland.

I have divided *Insight Pocket Guide: Gran Canaria* into two parts: (a) Las Palmas and the North and (b) the South, devising three full-day itineraries for the first and two full-day itineraries for the second, plus an assortment of optional excursions in each section to suit individual tastes. And although I hope to prise visitors off the islands' sand and send them in search of its soul, I have not neglected its justly famous beaches – child-tested by my own two girls.

Supporting the itineraries are essays on History and Culture, Eating Out and Shopping and a Practical Information section providing vital tips.

So get out there and explore, or else *el aplatanamiento* – which translates literally as 'the state of becoming a banana' might get you first. *Welcome – Bienvenido! — Margaret Hart*

CONTENTS

Welcome 5
History and Culture 12
Origins 13
Death of a Culture 14
Roots and Politics 15
A Bridge between Continents 16
Cosmopolitan Community 18
Historical Highlights 19

Day Itineraries 20

Las Palmas and the North
Day 1. City Sights 21
Day 2. To the Finger of God 28
Day 3. To the Top of the Island 33

Pick & Mix: The North
Option 1. Fontanales and Artenara 38
Option 2. Barranco de Guayadeque 41
Option 3. Las Palmas: Museums and Galleries 43
Option 4. Shopping in Las Palmas 46

The South
Day 4. Southern Beaches 49
Day 5. Inland 55

Pick & Mix: The South
Option 5. Palmitos Park and Maspalomas 58
Option 6. Water Sports and Fishing Trips 60

Shopping 62
Eating Out 64
Nightlife 68
Calendar of Special Events 71

Preceding pages: Sea and cliff at Puerto de las Nieves

Practical Information 74
Getting There 74
Travel Essentials 74
When to Go 74
Climate, Clothing, Documents 75
Electricity, Time Differences 76
Getting Acquainted 76
Geography, Government and Economy, Population and Religion 76
Money Matters 76
Tipping 77
Getting Around 77
Hours & Holidays 78
Accommodation 78
Cultural Events 79
Health & Emergencies 79
Crime 80
Sport 80
Maps 81
Toilets 81
Communications & News 81
Useful Addresses 81
Further Reading 81

Index 82

Maps

Gran Canaria IFC-1
The Canary Islands 2
Las Palmas 22–3
The North 28
Barranco de Guayadeque 42
Museums and Galleries 45
The South 50

Following pages: Camel Safari in the South

Histor

It is always difficult to separate the myth from the reality in the history and culture of the Canary Islands. Nobody is really clear what the Canary Islands were like before the 14th century, when the Spanish invaders finally put them on the geographical map and wiped the original Guanche culture off the face of the earth. If legend is anything to go by, Gran Canaria would appear to have been a kind of pastoral Arcadia. The Greeks and Romans wrote about the islands in glowing terms as the Hesperides, the Gardens of the Gods and Land of Eternal Spring and thereby, somewhat unwittingly, set them firmly on their way to

Myths – such as the tree which showered water – make up Canarian history

Culture

Dogs gave the islands their name

becoming the great tourist attractions they are nowadays.

Nor are the geological origins of the islands free from mythical interpretations. For many, the islands represent the remains of the sunken continent of Atlantis. A slightly more scientific hypothesis maintains that they are parts of Africa which broke away and drifted like ice floes in the shifting and sliding of the continents. The most extravagant of the hypotheses goes so far as to claim that the islands are the summits of a mountain chain which is still nosing its way upwards out of the Atlantic! What is known, however, is that they are volcanic islands, some of which are over 10 million years old.

Origins

The name, the 'Canary Islands', calls to mind the yellow singing birds we like to keep in cages – but don't expect to find them fluttering around here. There are all sorts of theories on the origin of the name, but singing birds don't feature. The most commonly held theory is that mentioned by Pliny in his description of an exploratory expedition sent by King Juba II of Mauretania to the island of Gran Canaria. The expedition brought back two enormous dogs, the *canes* of Canaria. That the locals share this theory is apparent in their coat-of-arms, emblazoned with two dogs, and the bronze sculptures of dogs which have been set up in the emblematic square of the Plaza de Santa Ana in Las Palmas.

However, there are no such doubts as to the origins of the 'Gran' in Gran Canaria. The heroic and stubborn defence of the island led the Spanish invaders to christen it 'Great'. For a long time, the Spaniards had found it impossible to conquer, largely due to the 14 local chieftains, the *guanartemes*, who fought together to stave off the enemy attacks. On the other Canary Islands the leaders were divided among themselves, making the Spaniards' job easier. Again, if legend is to be believed, this unity was the work of Princess Andamana of Gáldar, a woman of potent charm who seduced all 14 chieftains, thereby giving them something in common to fight for, and then married her blood brother to avoid rifts between her former suitors.

On the other islands, the Spaniards found conquest easier since the ladies tended to fall prey to their invaders' charms and helped them in their task – particularly on El Hierro.

Death of a Culture

On Gran Canaria, faced with the inevitability of their defeat, the *guanartemes* decided to end it all rather than live in slavery. Their method of death was as drastic as it was spectacular: they threw themselves off the highest rockfaces of the island. Those who survived the invasion quickly adapted to their new circumstances. The Guanches were, after all, a peace-loving, law-abiding race of cave-dwellers who divided their time between their community-tended fields and their herds of goats. Their two games of skill which were at all warlike in nature – the *juego del garrote* (two opponents armed with shepherds' crooks) and the *lucha canaria* (a kind of wrestling match) were only played to pass their leisure time when they were not singing or dancing. Their God was *Alcorán*, the God of the Sky, and their religion was based on fertility rites and rainmaking ceremonies. The two sacred mountains of Humiaga (now Cuatro Puertas: see *Day Itineraries*) and Tirma were used as *harimaguadas*, types of sanctuaries for the virgin daughters of nobility. Before being married off, these girls were taken to the grainstores such as the Cenobio de Valerón to be fattened up for the event. The women were highly important in the Guanche culture since it was through them that the race was perpetuated.

A Guanche mummy

According to legend, in Gomera and Gran Canaria it was customary for the man to gift his wife to a visiting guest in order to introduce new blood into the family.

The Spanish invaders described the Guanche men as exceedingly tall and the women as incredibly beautiful. However, it must be remembered that the average Spaniard of the time was no giant and that the soldiers had been a long time at sea without clapping eyes on a woman! The evidence does actually indicate that the Spaniards might have been right: mummies on display in the excellent Museo Canario in Las Palmas are around 1.84m (6ft) tall, certainly way above the average of the time.

The Spaniards brought Christianity

The process of mummification was highly elaborate and involved disembowelling the corpse, bathing it in shallow salt water (the Guanches apparently did not swim) then leaving it to dry, after which the body was wrapped up in goatskins and buried in one of a number of ways, depending upon social rank. The sap of the *drago*, the dragon tree indigenous to these islands, would also seem to have played an essential part in this ritual. Called 'dragon's blood' on account of its reddish colour, the sap was held to possess miraculous healing properties – which is perhaps just as well since the other predominant form of medical treatment was *trepanación* – a hole in the head.

Roots and Politics

To all intents and purposes, the culture of the Guanches disappeared after the Conquest and the subsequent incorporation of the island into the Spanish kingdom of the Catholic Monarchs, Ferdinand and Isabella, in 1478. Unfortunately there were no written records of the original language, which is thought to have been of Berber (African) origin. Canary Spanish is very different from mainland Spanish but this is only to be expected of islands that are nearer Africa than Spain and which have received influxes of people from all parts of the world. Moreover today's Canarios have also migrated to various parts of Latin America, above all Venezuela and Cuba, and later come back to their beloved islands. Words such as *naife* (a knife) or *guagua* (a bus) only exist here, so even mainland

Typical dress in the 1830s

Spaniards have difficulties at times in understanding the islanders.

Short-lived attempts have been made to dig out cultural roots and restore the lost Guanche identity, mainly by artists and intellectuals. The most important of these has been that of the Millares family, above all the painter Manolo Millares; also Martin Chirino, the sculptor, has incorporated the symbols of the *pintaderas* (the wooden or terracotta seals of the Guanches) into his work. Also playing their part have been Tony Gallardo, who works mainly with volcanic rock, and the partners Padorno and Lola Massieu.

Political movements of a nationalistic nature have never been very popular on this island. The political preferences of the people of Gran Canaria are thoroughly middle of the road; only the Central Democratic party, originally founded by the ex-Spanish President, Adolfo Suárez, maintained any kind of political foothold. In the early 1970s there was a spate of bomb scares mainly stage-managed by lawyer Antonio Cubillo and his radically nationalistic political party, MPAIAC. Exiled at the time in Algeria, Cubillo used to broadcast political propaganda over the radio and became an almost mythical figure. But democracy has changed all that and now Cubillo is considered an anecdotal and picturesque figure from the past.

Columbus is remembered here

A Bridge Between Continents

That the Canary Islands have long been important as a strategic port of call is evident from the fact that Columbus stopped off here at least once en route to America. The strong trading links which were established between the Canary Islands, Europe, America and Africa were to bring people of all nations to these shores. At the

Hotel patio from the early days of tourism

time when sugar cultivation was booming in the south of the island (at Agüimes and Ingenio for example) slaves were brought here, mainly by the Portuguese, from Africa. Thus, in Gran Canaria, there are two distinctly different strains of people: the tall, slender fair-skinned Canary islanders (the original Guanches were said to be redheads) and the swarthy, dark-skinned wiry-haired mainlanders. Although the ancient custom of gifting the wife to guests no longer exists, the effect of the 'new blood' of people from all parts of the world is apparent – above all in islands such as Fuerteventura where blonde-haired locals were non-existent before tourism.

The first and most important settlers were the British who originally came for reasons of health. One of the first tourist guides was Samler Brown's *Madeira, Canary Islands and Azores: A Practical and Complete Guide for the use of Tourists and Invalids* published in 1898. The British are held in great esteem by the Gran Canarians because their presence on the island has proved highly beneficial. For a long time Britain was the main foreign market for the principal exports from Gran Canaria, cochineal and wine. And when the other crops were blighted by plagues or foreign competition, the British introduced the cultivation of bananas and tomatoes.

Miller and Elder, whose warehouses still stand in the Parque Santa Catalina in Las Palmas, were largely responsible for opening up and developing the import-export trade which eventually prompted the Spanish government to nominate Las Palmas a Free Trade port. The water and electricity supplies were also set up by the British. Moreover, the second staple food of the Canary islanders (*gofio*, toasted cornflour, is the first) is the potato or *papa* which was grown from British seed – though an Englishman today would be hard-put to recognise the King Edward potato in the spud the Canaries call *papa kinewa*!

Cosmopolitan Community

Tourism, which represents a somewhat unbalanced 80 percent of the total income and employment of the island, has gradually brought people from all parts of the world to Gran Canaria – and a great many have stayed, attracted by the benign climate but, above all, by the easy-going pace of life and the hospitality of the local community. There are Japanese, German, British and French schools on the island – and even a community of Korean nuns. Although the times when the people of Gran Canaria left their front doors open at night or invited complete strangers to share their meals with them are very much things of the past, the most lasting impression that the tourist will take away is that of the extraordinary hospitality of this island.

Nevertheless, just as in the times of their forefathers, the people reveal a united front when faced with people who have come here merely to make a quick killing from the tourist business. These are given the derogatory title of *godos* (Goths) by the islanders and it is not unusual to see rubbish bins sprayed with the words *Godos aquí* ('Deposit Goths here').

Gran Canarians now view the current process of integration into the EC with mixed feelings: enthusiasm at belonging to the European Community – perhaps more than mainland Spaniards – yet forebodings at the economic consequences for the islands, which they fear the Community will ignore. As has always occurred in the past, they are likely to adapt cheerfully to the new set of circumstances and strive to maintain the quality of the peaceful life that they have long defended. Gran Canaria has the added status of the archipelago's capital city in Las Palmas – although the administration is shared with Santa Cruz in Tenerife.

Tourism produces 80 percent of island income

Historical Highlights

BC The Greeks and the Romans mentioned the Canary Islands in their texts. They referred to them as the *makaron nesoi*, the Gardens of the Hesperides, the Land of Eternal Spring and the Fortunate Islands. At that time, the islands were also probably known to the Phoenicians.

1st century AD Pliny wrote of the expedition sent to the islands by King Juba II of Mauretania. The expedition brought back two enormous dogs. No mention was made of the islands being inhabited though it is thought that the natives, the Guanches, may have hidden in caves to avoid detection, as has been proved in the case of the island of Lanzarote.

1367 The Canaries appear on a map for the first time.

1475–83 The island was constantly under attack, first by the Portuguese and then by the Spaniards under different leaders but financed by the Catholic Monarchs, Ferdinand and Isabella.

The whole island of Gran Canaria is held to have submitted to Pedro de Vera in 1483. This was largely due to the help of Tenesor Semidan, a *guanarteme* from the north who was captured, baptised a Christian under the name of Fernando Guanarteme and helped to convince his fellow islanders to surrender. Many of the other *guanartemes*, the local chieftains, threw themselves off the clifftops rather than submit.

1478 The first city, the Real de Las Palmas, was founded on Gran Canaria by the Crown of Castille.

1492 Christopher Columbus stopped off here on his first voyage to the New World. He repaired the rudder of *La Pinta* and the sail of *La Niña* (between the 25 August and the 1 September, according to the log-book). He was to return to Las Palmas on his second and fourth voyages.

15th and 16th centuries The Portuguese set up sugar plantations and mills in the South. They brought slaves from Africa. Attacks from Sir Francis Drake and the Dutch under Van der Hoes are repelled.

1526 Royal Tribunal established in Gran Canaria for the settlement of local disputes.

18th and 19th centuries The main exports are wine and cochineal. The British set up a Consulate on the islands from 1856 onwards. British settlers lay down the foundations of the import/export trade and play a large part in achieving water and electricity supplies. Coaling stations are set up in the harbour area to refuel transatlantic shipping.

1843 Benito Pérez Galdós, one of Spain's greatest novelists of all time, was born in Las Palmas de Gran Canaria.

1852 The islands are declared a Free Trade zone. First tourists arrive.

1870s Gran Canaria still only has barely ten miles of first-class road.

1927 The Canary Islands are divided into two provinces, East and West.

1936 Franco leaves Las Palmas for Spain and the Spanish Civil War begins.

1983 The Canary Islands are granted autonomous government but remain part of Spain.

1990 The island population reaches 600,000, with 355,000 living in the city of Las Palmas.

Day Itineraries

Gran Canaria is extraordinarily and naturally beautiful, but this beauty is not always instantly visible. The tourist may well feel distinctly un-seduced as the airport bus runs past barren landscapes dotted with cement plants and and necessary, but hardly picturesque, water purifying complexes towards Las Palmas de Gran Canaria; the road south of the airport to the resorts is no better, lined with skeletons of rudimentary plastic greenhouses. The grey colour of the houses is the result of a municipal tax: if you don't paint your house, you don't have to pay it.

But there is plenty to look forward to: as the bus rounds the corner after the dismal water-plant, Las Palmas de Gran Canaria lies stretched out along the coast, basking like a lazy lizard in the sun. Down South, the bus rounds the bend to reveal mile after mile of golden sands rolling away over the horizon. This is what Gran Canaria is all about.

For most of the following itineraries you should have your own transport. A convertible is not always totally practical for journeys inland or up north since there can be spectacular changes in temperature; a jeep allows you much more manoeuvrability but is not totally necessary unless you want to stray off the beaten track. In any case, be prepared. The roads into the interior twist and turn. The locals maintain that the Ministry of Works used donkeys to trace out the roads; you can see why they have come to that conclusion.

Gran Canaria's northern coast, with Las Palmas in the distance

Las Palmas & The North

Day 1

City Sights

Around Vegueta and along the old shopping street of Triana to the Pueblo Canario. Evening on Las Palmas' beach promenade at Las Canteras. Wear comfortable shoes for the cobblestones. On Tuesday and Sunday there are folk dances and songs in the Pueblo Canario. The majority of the museums are closed on Monday. Shops re-open at 4.30pm on Triana.

–To starting point: number 1 bus from Parque Santa Catalina to the end of the line: Teatro Pérez Galdós. Journey takes about 20 minutes.–

Las Palmas stretches along 9.5km (6 miles) of coast; this itinerary begins in the old part, and ends near the port in the commercial centre.

The **Teatro Pérez Galdós** is named after the famous Spanish realist novelist, Benito Pérez Galdós, born in Las Palmas. Alighting from your bus or taxi here, you are now at the crossroads

Casa de Colón

between **Triana**, one of the main shopping areas and **Vegueta**, the old quarter of the city and the original Real Las Palmas. Walk up past the theatre and cross over at the first pedestrian crossing. The road you are crossing used to be a fast-flowing river which, in times of heavy rainfall, occasionally threatened to sweep away the Puente de Piedra (the bridge no longer exists but once stood by the next pedestrian crossing up), which joined Triana to Vegueta and allowed the faithful to have access to the Cathedral on Sundays and feast days. On your left is the oldest of the local markets, on the corner of Mendizabal street, perhaps worth a visit on the way back if you are interested in tasting the local cheeses etc.

Turn along the second street on your right to catch the atmosphere of Vegueta: Calle Pelota is chock-a-block with old haberdasheries, ironmongers, antique shops and pet shops (including feathered canaries). At the end of the street, you face the erstwhile Cine Avellaneda, now the **Teatro Guiniguada** and used to host literary events (writers Tom Sharpe and John Fowles have both spoken here) and art seminars. Turn left past some of the oldest buildings in Las Palmas up to the back of the Cathedral where you will find the **Casa de Colón** (the House-Museum of Columbus: Monday to Friday 9.30am–5.30pm, Saturday 10am–1pm), worth a visit to

Canario and canary

see what Canary-style houses are like at their best and for the interesting artefacts and weapons of the time of the discovery of the Americas, together with the maps of the different voyages.

Coming out of the Casa de Colón, head along the street which borders the right side of the Cathedral (Calle Herrería) to come out onto the **Plaza Santa Ana**. This is the main square in Vegueta where you will find, at one end, the old **Town Hall** building and opposite, at the other end, the **Catedral Santa Ana**. It is almost *de rigueur* to have your photo taken beside the bronze dogs, the *canes* who gave their name to the Canary Islands. Sit beside them at the entrance to the square – one of the dogs was stolen not so many years ago by an enterprising thief; it was replaced but never recovered.

On Plaza Santa Ana

The Cathedral dominates the skyline in the old part of the city and, apart from being an obvious choice for photographers (especially when it is floodlit at night) it is well worth a visit. You have to enter by a door on the Calle Espíritu Santo, on the east side of the building. Since this is the entrance also to the **Museum of Religious Art** (Monday to Friday 9am–1.30pm and 4pm–6.30pm, Saturday 9am–2pm) you can visit both at the same time. This little museum, totally privately funded, houses a magnificent collection of Spanish colonial art. Unfortunately, its greatest treasures – leatherbound manuscripts and jewel-encrusted chalices and caskets – are not on public display since there are no glass cases

to exhibit them and the two highly enthusiastic young guides find it difficult to be in all places at once. However, in a side chapel of the Cathedral, you can see the famous *Pendón de la Conquista* (The Banner of the Conquest) embroidered by the Catholic Monarch, Queen Isabella herself. This side chapel is shared by the seemingly immortal remains of Bishop Codina who, quite honestly, looks a little the worse for wear.

Come out onto Calle Espíritu Santo and turn left behind the Cathedral to admire the balconies and the fountain in the square. From the square, turn down to the right to the Calle de los Balcones which, apart from being one of the most typical and well-kept streets in Vegueta and an obvious target for photographers, houses the CAAM (The Atlantic Centre of Modern Art, Tuesday–Saturday 10am–9pm; Sunday 10am–2pm). This centre, in conjunction with other museums and art galleries on the international circuit, organises exhibitions of enormous interest and together with the Reina Sofía in Madrid and the IVAM in Valencia, is one of the three main museums of modern art in Spain. The building itself is worth a visit to see how cleverly the traditional Canary architecture has been adapted to the needs of a modern art gallery.

Pérez Galdós in ston

Back up the cobbled pedestrian precinct of Calle de los Balcones and along to the right, past one of the oldest barber's shops in town and an interesting shop selling all kinds of religious statues of all shapes and sizes, you wind through a short narrow alleyway (Calle Algaba) to come out onto the square of the shrine/chapel of **San Antonio Abad** where, reputedly, Christopher Columbus heard

San Antonio Abad

Mass before setting off on his voyage of discovery. Opposite is a local handicraft shop where you will find some of the best (and cheapest) souvenirs in town, cheap because they are nearly all produced by prisoners in the local jail.

By now, you may be in need of a little light refreshment. Should you want to try a vegetarian restaurant (remember that Gran Canaria produces wonderful tomatoes, avocados, cucumbers, courgettes etc), you should make your way to **Hippocrates** which is along a narrow street (Colón) opposite San Antonio Abad. The restaurant is very close to the house where the famous Spanish tenor, Alfredo Kraus, was born and still lives when he is in town. Should you desire something more substantial, just a few yards along the road from the market, in the direction of the Calle de los Balcones, is **El Herreño** (Calle Mendizabal). Here you can sample the joys of *papas arrugadas con mojo* (small salty potatoes which you dip in a hot paprika-based sauce) and all the other regional delicacies at very decent prices.

After lunch, cross back over to **Triana** where you started but this time via the Alameda de Colón where you can admire the magnificent building of the **Gabinete Literario**. Wind your way right down the Calle Malteses until you come onto the street called Triana itself. Remember that the shops do not usually open until 4.30pm so, if you want to do something more than window-shop, take your time over lunch.

The pedestrian precinct here is full of interesting, good value shops, some of which have been established for years. Look out for the shopfront of **Metharam** with the carved wooden elephants' heads, and for the antique shop **Estoril** next door where real collectors' items are craftily hidden by their owner behind a barrage of cheap but colourful costume jewellery. **Maya** at the end of the road, on the corner with the **Parque San Telmo**, is perhaps the best value shop in town for cameras, electrical goods etc.

Kiosk on Parque San Telmo

At the far end of the Parque San Telmo, opposite the military headquarters from where Franco announced his military *coup* on the 18th July 1936, there is a delightful but dilapidated *art nouveau* kiosk which the local

Dancer at the Pueblo Canario

government has threatened to restore on more than one occasion. If you are feeling energetic, you can stroll along León y Castillo, passing by the **Plaza de la Feria** where there is a fearful statue of Pérez Galdós framed against the background of the **Gobierno Civil** (watch out for the Civil Guards with their typical *tricornios*, three-cornered hats) and opposite, the **Comandancia Marina**. You should bear in mind that the building of the Comandancia Marina used to be on the seafront and, therefore, that all the buildings along the **Avda Marítima** are built on land reclaimed from the sea. The harbour area was formerly situated around this end of the town and, therefore, there is a traditional red-light district here, though the 'ladies of leisure' are definitely in the veteran league.

Continue along León y Castillo for the **Pueblo Canario** (the Canary Village) which is some 20 minutes' walk from Triana. It is not a particularly scenic walk, so if you are feeling tired, jump into a taxi. The Pueblo Canario, in the grounds of the magnificent **Hotel Santa Catalina** (one of the oldest and most emblematic buildings in Las Palmas) was designed by the famous Canary painter Néstor de la Torre and built by his brother, Manuel Martín Fernández de la Torre. The **Museum of Néstor de la Torre** (Tuesday–Friday 10am–1pm and 4pm–8pm, Sunday 11am–1pm), in the Pueblo Canario is well worth a visit. Behind the **Bodegón** (another excellent place to eat) in the Pueblo, there is a park which was once a mini-zoo, with lions and bears, but which now only sports two tired turtles. In front of the hotel is a statue commemorating the fall of the original local chieftains, the *guanartemes*, who, rather than submit to Spanish rule, threw themselves off the cliffs.

Take a late afternoon drink of local rum (*Arehucas-Carta de Oro*) and coke on the verandah of the Hotel Santa Catalina and browse around the shops in the Pueblo Canario where, if nothing else, you can view a representative sample of everything which is typical of Gran Canaria (*timples*, a musical instrument like a tiny guitar, *naifes*, Canary knives, embroidered tablecloths and typical Canary costumes). Then you can either stroll a little further along to the **British Club** to see where the expats congregate near the end of León y Castillo, next door to what used to be the Hotel Metropole and is now the Town Hall, and then back along the seafront to the

Las Canteras, the city-centre beach

Parque Santa Catalina and a well-earned rest in the park itself or on the **Paseo de las Canteras**, the beach front promenade from where, if the day is clear, you will see the sun setting over Mount Teide in Tenerife. If the whole day has been too strenuous already, then take a taxi back to the hotel.

An evening dip is an essential experience in Las Palmas, and Las Canteras beach is one of the finest to be found in the whole of Spain, even though it is within the city itself. After your swim, since the day has already been rather long and hard on the feet, stroll along the Paseo de las Canteras towards the Hotel Imperial Playa end (that is, towards the east) where, next door to the hotel, you will find **Casa Carmelo**. This restaurant looks out over the sea and is excellent for meat (try their *solomillo* – sirloin) or fish (try the *sama* – sea bream or the *viejas* – parrotfish!). You're not driving anywhere so indulge in a good wine; if you like white, try the local El Grifo from Lanzarote, a malmsey which comes in three versions with the medium-dry possibly the best. If you still feel active, stroll back towards the Hotel Meliá where in the basement, you will find **El Coto**, a disco frequented by the older generation in Las Palmas (which here means everybody over 21!). Or if you feel in the mood for something more romantic and mellow, the piano-bar on the first floor of the same hotel offers a spectacular view over the beach and the accompaniment of the Cuban pianist who will play all your favourite tunes. Then have a nightcap of *cubalibre* (made with the wonderful Cuban Habana Club rum) and a stroll back along the beach to your hotel.

Dominoes in Parque Santa Catalina

DAY 2

To the Finger of God

Via Guía and Gáldar to Reptilandia and the Dedo de Dios (God's Finger). Back via the Valle de Agaete. With stops en route, this itinerary takes approximately 6 hours. The road is fairly straightforward with no great bends until you are in the Valle de Agaete. Remember that you will be changing altitude – Los Berrazales is 400m (1,312ft). Puerto de las Nieves is a pebble beach so take appropriate footwear.

–To starting point: Drive up Luis Morote, past Parque Santa Catalina and turn left at end along Bernardo de la Torre. Turn right at the first traffic lights and you are on Guanarteme.–

Drive out of Las Palmas on Guanarteme. At the end, you will see the road to the north (Norte) clearly signposted. Drive out along the C-810, stopping off briefly at **El Rincón**, to admire the view and the impressive volcanic rock sculpture, *Atlanta*, by the Canary artist Tony Gallardo. Be careful not to stray too close to the edge of the rocks here since the site is badly cared for and the fence has

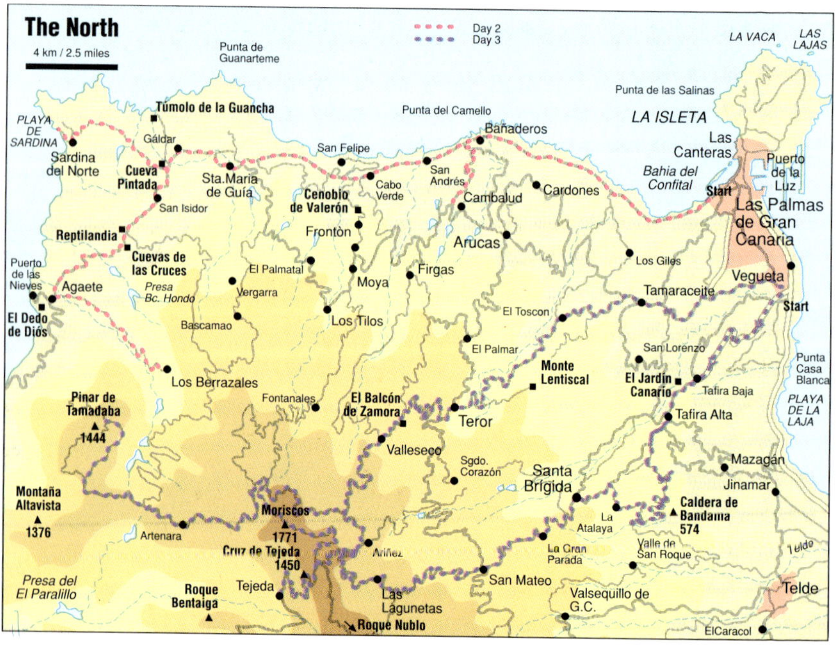

been knocked away in some places.

The road out through San Andrés and Bañaderos is hardly what you would call exciting although the view over the saltpans (Las Salinas) just outside **Bañaderos** is worth a stop and a photograph (where you see the sign 'Tiro Olímpico – 9km', pull off to the right). Just before the spectacular soaring bridge of Puente de Silva is a turning off to the left which you reach via a roundabout; the road winds up to the **Cenobio de Valerón** (signposted) one of the few archaeological sites open to the public but ever more in danger of being closed. The steps up to this Guanche granary hewed out of the rock are extremely perilous and you will receive no help from the attendant, who is fairly old and taciturn, nor for that matter will you receive any information. Looking out from this viewpoint, you can see the high rock from which, allegedly, the last *guanarteme*, Bentejuí, threw himself. (See *History and Culture* section). The Puente de Silva is bedecked with wire netting to prevent contemporary Canary islanders from emulating him.

Cenobio de Valerón

Once back in the car on the C-810, you will notice if you look down from the bridge and observe the wayside crops after the series of tunnels, that you are approaching the banana plantation area of the island.

Local crop

You will now pass through the two rival towns of **Guía,** famous for its rennet cheese (*Queso flor de Guía*) and **Gáldar**, the pre-Spanish capital of Gran Canaria. On the road between the two on the left-hand side, shortly before entering Gáldar, stand the **Leacock** buildings, testimony to the beneficial influence of the British on this island. Leacock was one of the British settlers who started up the banana export industry. On his death, he bequeathed the whole business to his workers (it has since gone bankrupt). Gáldar, like Guía before it, is not enormously impressive but you should visit the **Cueva Pintada** (well signposted but very bad for parking space) which is decorated with

Cave house, Sardina del Norte

the geometric drawings also to be found on the prehistoric Guanche *pintaderas* (terracotta and wooden seals which are believed to have been used either to tattoo the body or to identify different families' stores of grain). The other archaeological site, lately restored, is the **Túmulo de la Guancha** (a Guanche necropolis) which is reached via the scariest narrow road off the main plaza, bordered by high breeze-block walls. Just behind the site of the Túmulo is a natural rock-pool which is used by the locals as a swimming pool. This is the place for a quick dip.

Just beyond Gáldar, a road forks off to the west, towards **Sardina del Norte**. This small fishing village has a charming beach which is magnificent for underwater swimming and snorkelling. If you take the road as far as it goes, you will come to a restaurant, perched on the rocks, where the fish and seafood is kept in wide open tanks full of constantly running water. If you are not too hungry, take a snack or a *tapa* here then head back to the main road (C-810) and on to Agaete.

At the crossroads with Hoya de Pineda, you will see the signpost for **Reptilandia** (Monday to Sunday 11am–5.30pm), a reptile park run by a British couple and their Canary partner. Here you can see chameleons, lizards, giant tortoises and crocodiles in open enclosures which strongly resemble their natural habitat. The monkeys, tarantulas, poisonous toads, snakes, and the latest acquisition, the hissing cockroaches, are all either in cages or in glass cases. But you *can* enjoy the sensation of being embraced in the coils of Monty the python and find out that snakes are not at all slimy.

Reptiland

Back on the C-810, the road winds on down past the **Cuevas de las Cruces**, a set of caves on the left-hand side of the road which are good for a photograph (unfortunately they seem to have been used as makeshift loos for bus trips), past the inhabited cave houses on the right-hand side of the road and into **Agaete**. You should turn down to the right, down behind the Church of **La Concepción** (17th century) where the signpost indicates **Puerto de las Nieves**. This is a small fishing village with a pebbly beach and with one of the most characteristic views of Gran Canaria: the rocky outcrop known as **El Dedo de Dios** (God's Finger). Park wherever you can in the square but try to avoid leaving your vehicle too close to the camels and the donkeys which provide rides for the young and the not so young.

There are several excellent restaurants in Puerto de las Nieves but perhaps the best is also called **El Dedo de Dios**, from which you can view the famous rock. Puerto de las Nieves is well-known for many things, amongst which are the hilarious blunders made in the translations of the restaurant menus, though with the implementation of Translation Studies in the University of Las Palmas, things are gradually changing for the better. In any case, do not be worried by 'rape sailor-style' since what they are really offering you is *rape a la marinera* (a local fish with a herby sauce garnish)!

El Dedo de Dios (God's Finger)

After lunch, stroll along the Paseo de los Poetas. Then, before going back to the car, drop in to the **Ermita de las Nieves** which boasts a magnificent 16th-century Flemish triptych, recently restored.

Drive back to Agaete and take the road to the east signposted **El Valle**. The road gradually winds its way up through this incredibly beautiful valley, past **La Casa Romántica** (wonderful for coffee and cakes and soon to be the site of an 'adventure holiday' hotel) until you come to the hotel at **Los Berrazales**. Be warned! The bend just before the hotel, immediately after

the water bottling factory, is a really scary one, especially if you meet the local bus coming down, so take care. There used to be a spa at Los Berrazales but even though this no longer exists, the view down the valley is an exhilarating experience in itself.

Only the truly adventurous should continue up this road, which peters out at El Sao before the Pinar de Tamadaba, but which affords heady views. Otherwise, take the same road back down, after some light refreshment of course, and back to Las Palmas.

The neo-Gothic San Juan Bautista

To introduce something new on the way back, take the road off to the right just before Bañaderos, signposted **Arucas**. Here you should twist your way up the Montaña to be rewarded by another magnificent view over the neo-Gothic church of **San Juan Bautista** (sometimes wrongly referred to by the locals as 'the Cathedral' on account of its size) and over the bay of Las Palmas. There is a restaurant on the top of the hill, so you can sip a drink of Tia Maria liqueur whilst enjoying the view. Then back to Las Palmas via the main road (C-810).

In the evening, treat yourself to something completely different. **El Hamburgo** (Tel: 222745), as the name indicates, is a German restaurant in Calle Mari Sánchez. Again you stroll east along Las Canteras beach past the Hotel Imperial Playa and when the beachfront walk ends, you turn up to the right, up Mari Sánchez (formerly called General Orgaz) where you will see the restaurant on the right hand side of the road. The Canary owner Manolo and his German wife will give you a night to remember, with all the best in German cuisine brightened by Manolo's repartee. He speaks at least five languages fluently and is dreadfully mischievous in all five. Save some space for the scrumptious desserts.

Manolo in El Hamburgo

After dinner, stroll back down onto the beachfront and, before the Hotel Imperial Playa, turn left down the Calle Ferrera where you will see **La Posada** on your right. Here, you will find all the combinations of coffee with liqueurs that you could possibly imagine.

DAY 3

To the Top of the Island

This six-hour itinerary goes via the Jardín Canario up to the Pinar de Tamadaba (which is 1,444m (4,737ft) above sea level so take warm clothing). Spectacular views all the way along a route that takes in La Atalaya, San Mateo and Artenara. The local Fiestas 'del Almendro en flor' – to celebrate the flowering of almond-trees – are usually held at the end of January.

–To starting point: Drive along the Avda. Marítima and turn off to the left at the flyover/Pérez Galdós theatre. From there take the c-811 to Tafira. See map on p28.–

The road up to Tafira is commonly referred to as the 'Scalextric route' for its many horrible bends and for the speed of its traffic. Look out for the two bends just beyond the Tropical (local beer) factory. Drive straight up the Llano de las Brujas where, if you look down to the right, you will see the old folks' home. Move into the right-hand lane, even at the risk of getting caught behind one of the UTINSA buses (slow-moving and disgusting exhaust-pipe fumes), past the University campus in Tafira Baja and look out for the sign which indicates the **Jardín Canario**, the first stop.

Park outside the restaurant and enter the gardens by the top gate. Work your way down through the grounds admiring the magnificent collection of local flora on show including the legendary *dragos*, the dragon-trees, and the cactus garden. Unfortunately, the hike back to the car is no stroll but reward yourselves at the top with a local beer (Tropical of course) and goat's cheese (*queso tierno*) at the restaurant, **El Jardín Canario**. There are magnificent views from the closed balcony.

Suitably refreshed, climb back into the car. Take care leaving the gardens since cars whizz along this part of the road at great speed and you

Beware of pedestrians on the Tafira road

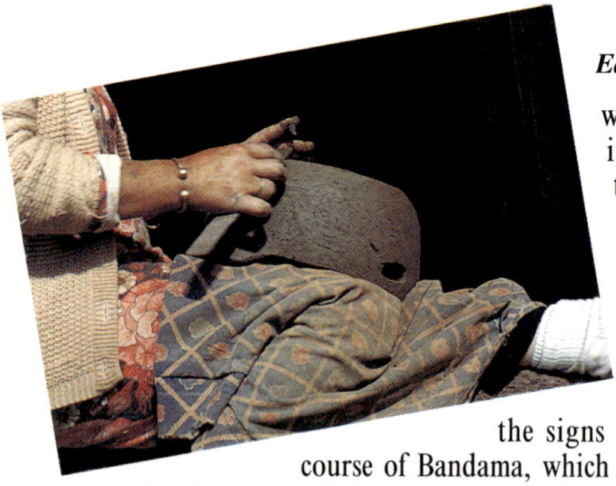

Earthenware

will also have to move over into the left-hand lane, the fast lane, as soon as possible. Continue up through the narrow part of Tafira, past one of the first hotels on the island, Los Frailes, on your left and follow the signs which indicate the golf course of Bandama, which is perched on top of the volcanic crater of the same name. The **Caldera de Bandama**, at 574m (1,889ft) offers spectacular views over Las Palmas. If you look hard, you will notice that there is a house nestled down at the foot of the crater. The old man who lives there climbs up and down every day and, logically enough, has no problems either with robbers or with his animals escaping!

The **Golf Club of Bandama** was founded by the British community, which still tends to centre around Tafira since the climate is cooler and wetter and reminds them more of home. It is the oldest golf club in the whole of Spain (set up in 1891) and its nine holes are very carefully tended. Golf is now an up-and-coming sport in Spain, with the Ballesteros and Olazábals of the world blazing trails of glory. The Caldera is also a favourite haunt of courting couples – perhaps because it is cooler up here; watch out for oddly parked cars.

Roads here are narrow and twisting

A road runs along the side of the golf course, past the British School and the riding school to the cave village of **La Atalaya**, famous for its earthenware pottery which is hand-moulded and left to bake in the sun. The most famous of the potters, Panchito, died a few years ago but his disciples make sure that his memory lives on. To enter the village turn right at the crossroads and then up to the left and the best views and best pottery are to be found down a flight of steps behind the village square where the church stands.

Once back in the car, and if you feel adventurous, you should follow the narrow road up behind the church. A very rudimentary traffic-light, which works highly efficiently nonetheless, controls the traffic up to **La Concepción**, one of the most exclusive sites for a house on the island thanks to its magnificent views. The little shrine on the left, now almost abandoned to its fate, is the oldest *ermita* on the island.

Back down the slope and turn down to the left beside the church square. Left again will take you down the Carretera de la Atalaya (where I live) to the main road. Turn left at the crossroads but be careful because visibility to the right is very poor. You will now pass through **Santa Brígida** where Dutch invaders, under Van der Hoes, were driven back and out of Gran Canaria by the islanders in 1599. Continue on the C-811, running past Pino Santo on the right and the old British country club, now a restaurant called Monte Verde, on your left. A little farther up the road, on the left, in a place called El Madroñal you will see the restaurant **Martel** (open every day). The owner of this typical Canary restaurant also has one of the best wine-cellars on the whole of the island and offers a wide variety of cheeses and olives in *mojo* (a herby sauce).

Roadside shrine

Back in the car, continue up the road to **San Mateo** where, shortly after an incongruously ugly statue presumably representing the noble peasant, on the right, you will see the ethnological museum of **Cho Zacarías** (closed Sunday and local holidays; Monday to Saturday 9.30am–1pm. Entrance fee). This is well worth an unhurried visit so if there are coaches parked outside, take a stroll first round the village and look in at the **Pastelería San Mateo**, just a little farther up the pavement, where you will be able to buy the delicious *bienmesabe*, a sticky honey and almond sauce. The local market is along the first road on your left so have a stroll round it to see what the natives eat.

You should have your lunch in the restaurant in Cho Zacarías (closed Monday) so make sure you give yourself time to look round the museum first. The restaurant is also decorated with typical farming implements. Look out for the enormous bellows beside the fireplace! The food is all delicious and the owner, who speaks both English and German, will be pleased to recommend dishes.

After lunch, prepare for the winding, hair-raising drive up through the mountains (there is a particularly nasty bend at La Lechuza) to **Cruz de Tejeda** at 1,450m (4,757ft) following the signposts. The cross is one of many different types to be seen at different high-standing locations in order to mark the supremacy of Christianity. The **Parador**, a kind of castle-like construction, is worth a visit, above all to take photos of **Roque Nublo, Roque Bentaiga** and **El Fraile**, three spectacular volcanic rock outcrops, from the terrace. You may want to take a drink and a rest here since you have changed altitude very abruptly and may be feeling it.

For those of you who are not exhausted already and are keen photographers, go back onto the C-811, back the way you came until you come to a fork signposted for **Artenara** (see *Pick and Mix* section). The road to Artenara is one long bend around gorges and terraced landscapes but affords wonderful views. The village itself is tiny. Just before the village square down to the right, you will see a signpost for **La Silla**. This restaurant is entered via a tunnel, at the end of which you will be welcomed by the most spectacular view, weather permitting of course, of Roque Nublo and the Bentaiga. This restaurant is well worth visiting on its own so those of you who have not stayed the pace should not despair since it is included in another itinerary in this book.

Back in the car, continue along the same road which winds its way up to the dizzy heights of the **Pinar de Tamadaba**, 1,444m (4,737ft). Here in this spectacular pine forest you are assured of spectacular views over Agaete and also of Mount Teide on Tenerife, if the day is clear.

Photographers should make their way back to Las Palmas via **Valleseco** (well signposted). In Valleseco itself, if you have not already taken enough breathtaking pictures, the restaurant on the right-hand side of the road, **El Balcón de Zamora**, offers you the possibility for a few more.

The next stop on this winding road is the village of **Teror** (GC-230 again, well signposted). Teror is good for a leisurely stroll to admire the incredible wooden balconies and typical Canary architecture. The recently re-opened **Casa-Museo de los Manrique** is also well worth a visit to see how the island's upper echelons used to live! (open 11am– 7.30pm). Also good in Teror is the **Basilica de**

Typical balcony in Teror

View of Bentaiga

Nuestra Sra del Pino, the Baroque-neoclassic temple which houses the **Virgen del Pino**, patroness of the island. A door behind the altar will allow you to get a closer glimpse of the statue of the Madonna, decked out in precious jewellery (which has been stolen on more than one occasion) gifted to the church by devotees who have had their prayers answered. On 8 September each year (see *Calendar of Special Events*) people from all over the islands set off in groups to walk, or even crawl on their knees, along the road to the shrine.

Opposite the Basilica, different stalls peddle their wares in the main square (there is a street market on Sunday) and a rather downtrodden-looking bar offers the possibility of tasting the delights of the *chorizo de Teror* (a highly spiced sausage whose memory lingers on your breath quite a while afterwards) and *turrón* (a kind of soft nougat made from *gofio*). If you feel really brave, try the local rum as the natives drink it: on its own.

The road from Teror back to Las Palmas is fairly fast at first; after **Tenoya** it is narrow and winding. It then goes through Tamaraceite and back into **Las Palmas** via the Feria del Atlántico. If you look up to the left, at the second traffic lights, you will see the Feria: the Trade Fair precinct. (The Trade Fair takes place in April every year.) Continue straight down the hill, keeping in the left-hand lane round the back of the football stadium and straight down to the Plaza de España. Turn second right off the roundabout and down Mesa y López, past the department stores Galerías Preciados. Follow this street as far as it goes and, at the end, turn left for the Parque Santa Catalina and familiar surroundings.

Teror's Virgen del Pino

Reward yourself at the end of this long day with a relaxing drink on the terrace of the **Hotel Meliá** on the Paseo de las Canteras (bearing east) and then dinner in the beautifully decorated restaurant **El Jardín Botanico** in the same hotel, with its magnificent views over the beach. And if you are still not tired, then make for **Pachá**, a disco (Calle Simón Bolívar) along from the Elder and Miller buildings on Parque Santa Catalina or enjoy the balmy night with a last drink on a terrace bar in the Parque itself.

Pick

Option 1. Fontanales and Artenara

A morning excursion into the interior via Moya, incorporating the museum of an island poet, pine and laurel forests and a holy shrine. Especially recommended for those who missed out Artenara on Day 3. A jeep is essential for the stretch which takes you through the Tilos de Moya to Fontanales.

–To starting point: leave Las Palmas via Guanarteme. *See map on p. 28.–*

Moya

After Guanarteme, take the road to the north (C-810). It runs along the coast but is marred by haphazard building work (islanders leave their properties unpainted in order to avoid the hefty taxes levied on finished buildings). Run through **Bañaderos** and take the turning off to the right, signposted **Pagador**. Follow the road round the bend, past a church with a painted representation of a stained-glass window and take the road signposted for **Moya**, which passes through **Cabo Verde**, steep in parts and extremely narrow in others but affording fine views. The road enters Moya from below the square, where a fine church hangs perilously over the cliff-face (you can take a great photo from here right down the gully to the sea). Across from the square stands the **House-Museum of Tomás Morales**, one of the most famous poets of the Canary Islands (daily from 10am–2pm, closed holidays).

Follow the road round the bottom of the church and up to the right. This street takes you past the ladies selling *suspiros* (meringues) and *bizcochos* (sponge fingers), typical of Moya but not recommended if you are running a healthy thirst, and down to a crossroads. If you want an easy run up to Fontanales, turn up to the left, where the town is signposted. Otherwise, and only if you are driving a jeep, continue straight on and take the next turning off to the left where **Los Tilos de Moya** is signposted. Much of this laurel forest has been closed to the public in an effort to halt environmental damage. The road (always open) is not often used and you can tell why; proceed slowly as it is narrow as well as winding and cars may come down in the opposite direction, often on a steep incline. However, the countryside is beautiful and the sense of travelling through parts of

Moya street

Biking at Earthways

the island that even the natives do not know is exhilarating.

Fontanales is a typical Canary village nestling in a valley between volcanic hills. If you have come via Los Tilos, you turn left at the main road and enter Fontanales the back way, past the church. Otherwise, you come in on the main road. Park near the **Restaurante Sibora** or the **Bar Fontanales**, good places in which to adjourn for a drink and a *tapa* (animal lovers are warned: the Bar Fontanales is adorned with the proud owner's hunting trophies).

Back on the road, on the right about 1km (½ mile) further on, is **Earthways,** a typical Canary farmstead run by a British couple who organise adventure and activity holidays. It's worth dropping in to see what's on offer.

Regaining the main road, follow the signposts to **Artenara**. Here I recommend you have lunch in the **Mesón de la Silla** which, besides serving good, decent-priced food in pleasant surroundings, offers those who didn't follow the *Day 3* itinerary the opportunity to photograph the peaks of **Roque Nublo** and **Roque Bentaiga** from the verandah. Artenara itself is little more than a square but a little road up beside the church (best travelled on foot) will take you to the quaint grotto of the **Virgen de la Cuevita**, site of an annual procession (see *Calendar of Special Events*).

Suitably refreshed, you can either drive back to Las Palmas, taking the route via **San Mateo** and **Santa Brígida** (the C-811) which you came up on *Day 3*, or, if you have time to spare (roughly one hour there and back) and did not choose the alternative route on *Day 3*, continue on to the **Pinar de Tamadaba** (1½km/1 mile), the incredible pine forest which towers above Agaete and affords fine views of Mount Teide on Tenerife provided of course the day is sufficiently clear.

Whether you choose to go to the Pinar or not, you can return via **Hoya de Pineda** (slightly farther along the road from Artenara in the direction of Tamadaba), **Montaña Vergara,** back down past the Cenobio de Valerón (see *Day 1*) and on to the main road back to Las Palmas via Bañaderos. The second option is hair-raising at times but the views are magnificent.

Option 2. Barranco de Guayadeque

A half-day excursion to the deep ravine (Barranco) of Guayadeque via the windswept regions of Telde and Ingenio. Lunch in a cave restaurant in the Barranco where, on Sunday, holidays and other busy times, you can sample 'sancocho', a special fish dish.

–To starting point: Drive down Calle Nicolás Estevanez, past Parque Santa Catalina. Cross over Leon y Castillo at the traffic lights and turn third right to connect with the motorway down to the South (GC-1). Jeep advisable.–

Caves at Cuarto Puertas

Leave **Las Palmas** by the road for the airport and turn off where you see Telde signposted. **Telde**, *la ciudad de los muebles* (the city of furniture), has more furniture shops per square metre than any other town on the islands. Telde is also famous for its faith-healers, its superstitions and the fact that its inhabitants have won the Christmas national lottery prize (known as *El Gordo* or the fatty) more times than anywhere else in Spain including Madrid and Barcelona. Together with Gáldar, Telde was the main centre for the original Guanches and the site of the discovery of the emblematic *ídolo de Tara*, one of their cherished idols.

If you can find a parking space, the church of **San Juan** merits a visit, especially on account of its strange crucifix made out of corncobs mounted on silver (Luján Pérez). The district of **San Francisco**, across the road, is also worth a stroll since here you can see

Looking down the Barranco

the most representative collection of Canary-style houses on the island. Back in the car, take the road for **Los Llanos** (C-812) to visit **Cuatro Puertas** site of one of the original *harimaguadas* (see *History and Culture page 14*).

Continue down the C-812 past **Aguatona** towards Ingenio, named after the Portuguese for sugar-mill. This region was famous for its sugar-cane production, although it is much diminished nowadays. Just outside Ingenio, you should not miss **El Museo de Piedras** (daily 9am–6pm) which has a fascinating display of old farm tools and, as the name suggests, rocks. It also boasts a representative display of local handicrafts.

Back in the car, continue into Ingenio. At the crossroads, on the corner, you may see the locals selling *morenas*, big electric eels which are considered a great delicacy. It is worth turning right, where the **Barranco de Guayadeque** is signposted, then right again and into the town square. **Ingenio** was a town largely founded by the Portuguese and has inherited a tradition of witchcraft and superstition from the large slave population which inhabited it for a long time.

The road to the Barranco twists its way up then plunges suddenly downwards. The Barranco is most representative of what the Guanches' territory used to be like. The cliffs are dotted with caves hacked out of the walls, some for human habitation, others for housing goats.

Continue along the road to the right, winding up to the restaurant, itself housed in a maze of caves, which offers you, again, a breath-

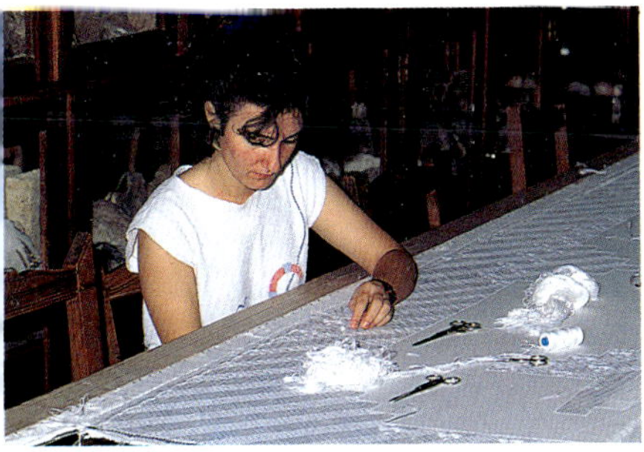

Lacemaker in El Museo de Piedras

taking view down the gully. Here you can get typical Canary food. On Sunday and holidays the restaurant serves *sancocho* (salted fish served with boiled sweet potatoes and *mojo* with an accompaniment of *gofio* kneaded with milk and bananas – the speciality of the region); it is the only restaurant still to serve it. If you try it make sure you drink plenty of water or beer.

From the Barranco, wend your way down to **Agüimes**, whose carnival celebrations are said to beat any on the islands, down through **Vecindario** (formerly tomato-producing country) called *la ciudad de los Mercedes* on account of the of rich people who live there. Regain the main road back to Las Palmas, leaving behind the beaches of **Melenara**, **Playa del Hombre** and **La Garita**, small, badly maintained beaches which do not merit a stop-off unless you are desperately hot and dusty.

Option 3. Las Palmas: Museums and Galleries

Most tourists to Gran Canaria are unaware of the wide-ranging selection of art galleries and museums which are open to them and, with the weather so good, few people bother to find out. But if you want to take an afternoon off from sun-bathing there is plenty to see in the stimulating collections in Las Palmas de Gran Canaria. I suggest that you hop between these by taxi or bus (Lines 1 and 2 take you to Vegueta from the Parque Santa Catalina) since parking is a problem.

The best small museum, without a shadow of a doubt, is the **Museo Canario**, Calle Dr Chil, Vegueta (Monday to Friday, 10am–1pm and 4–7.30pm, Saturday 10am–1pm, Sunday 10am–2pm). It rates at least an hour's visit. Here you have one of the best collections of mummies in the world (recognised as such in the last unlikely-sounding International Mummy Congress, held in Puerto de la Cruz, Tenerife, in 1991). You can also see the vestiges of the pre-Conquest culture of the Guanches – their *pintaderas* (see *History and Culture*); their idols (*el ídolo de Tara*), strongly reminiscent of monuments associated with fertility rites to be found in Cornwall, England – and find out about the islands'

Home to a fine museum

Guanche mummy remains in the Museo Canario

customs. For example, did you know that the most common remedy for illness among the Guanches was *trepanación*, boring a hole in the head of the patient? Or that they could not swim? Or that the female sexual apparatus was so revered that it was painted over the walls of caves? The novelist John Fowles described the museum when he was here in 1991 as 'one of the finest small museums I have ever had the fortune to visit.' For the more studious, the Museo Canario also boasts an impressive library containing the original writings of the Marquis of Bute, who was one of the Canaries' first tourists.

A little farther up the Calle Dr Chil, on the right, is the **Square of Santo Domingo**, another significant spot in Vegueta. It was here that the Guanches formally submitted to the Spanish invaders in the presence of the famous Banner of the Conquest (see *Day 1*). Walk back down the far side of the church on the square, across Plaza Santa Ana and past the restoration work on the Episcopal Palace across from the Cathedral. Cross at the traffic lights.

On the far corner, opposite the Alameda de Colón (once an avenue lined with trees) you will find the CICA, the art gallery cum museum/conference centre run by the Caja de Ahorros (Savings Bank), another good venue for exhibitions. Retrace your steps and cross over to the other pavement at the traffic lights for the so-called **Plaza de las Ranas** (the Square of the Frogs – you should see why). You ought to be able to resist the smell of roast chicken and garlic potatoes at this time of day but the Baskin-Robbins ice-cream shop may be too much of a temptation. Ice-cream in hand, stroll down to the left past the recently re-opened **Biblioteca Insular** (Monday to Friday 10am–1pm and 4–8pm). This library is one of the best examples of late 19th-century architecture in Las Palmas.

Make your way down the Calle Peregrina – look out for the artisan carpenter's next to the old printer's – and out onto the Calle Malteses. If you turn up to the left here, you will find an interesting haberdashery/lingerie shop selling all kinds of unusual under-

The Pérez Galdós Museum

wear. Otherwise, turn down to the right, then first left for the Calle Cano and the **Casa-Museo Benito Pérez Galdós** (Monday to Friday 9am–1pm and 4–8pm). Considered one of the greatest Spanish novelists of all time and the ultimate exponent of realism in Spanish literature, Pérez Galdós was born and lived in this somewhat unpretentious house from 1843 to 1862. Of his work, his novels *Fortunata* and *Jacinta* are published in English by Penguin Classics.

Stroll along Calle Cano until it meets Viera y Clavijo. Along the way, observe the variety of architectural styles in this district, in particular the splendid examples of art nouveau and modernism. Look out for **Sayme** and **Madelca**, both of which sell prints of modern Canary artists. In Viera y Clavijo, you will find the tempting cake-shop and delicatessen **Morales**. If you are in the mood for something savoury, try a *sandwich de berros* (a water-cress sandwich). There are so many delicious sweets to choose from, it is difficult to recommend any in particular but I suggest you try the San Marcos for size.

Stroll up Bravo Murillo to see the classic modernist building of the **Cabildo,** beside which is the **Centro Insular de Cultura** (Monday to Friday 9am–2pm and 5–8pm), where you are sure to find an exhibition of traditional crafts, photography, art or architecture.

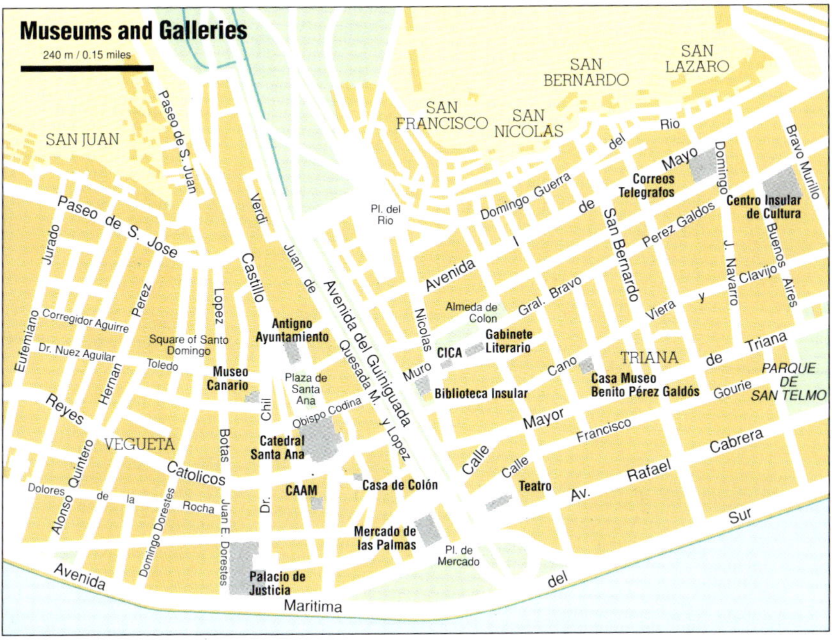

You might be lucky!

Cross at the traffic lights to catch a bus on the corner, past the bookshop **Librería Nogal**, where you can pick up books on the islands as well as English paperbacks. Just before catching the bus, though, cross over to a shop called **Art-Décor,** where you will find the best in Canary sculpture, art and crafts, all duly authenticated.

If you prefer to take a taxi rather than a bus, hail it on this side of the road. Cross back for the bus and buy a lottery ticket, the *ciegos* (so-called because it is run by ONCE, the Spanish Organisation for the Blind, one of the richest and most influential charities in the world). You never know – you might strike lucky!

From the Parque Santa Catalina, walk back to **La Regenta** (Calle León y Castillo, 427. Monday to Friday 11am–1pm and 6–9pm) which offers a variety of excellent exhibitions by Canary artists and photographers.

Option 4. Shopping in Las Palmas

Breakfast on Parque Santa Catalina followed by best buys – from silk blouses to electric gadgets – in Las Canteras.

Las Palmas is a duty-free port, so you can find goods from all parts of the world here and at bargain prices. There are three main shopping areas. The first, where I suggest you spend the morning, lies in the part of Las Palmas behind Parque Santa Catalina (between the port and the beach) which is commonly referred to as **Las Canteras**. The second is **Triana** where the Canary islanders shop and where the most 'typical' souvenirs related to Canary culture can be bought (see *Day 1*). The third is the area around **Mesa y López**, halfway between Triana and Las Canteras and dominated by the two big department stores, **El Corte Inglés** and **Galerías Preciados**. This is the best place to shop for clothes.

Las Canteras offers something for everybody, including friends back home. Start off with a fortifying breakfast on one of the terraces on the **Parque Santa Catalina**. Ask for *chocolate con churros* which you dunk into the thick hot chocolate – a typically Spanish start to the day.

Street sales

After breakfast, set off up the **Calle Ripoche**, off the middle of the square. This is 'haggling' territory where you can pick up real bargains if you know how to strike a mean deal. Most of these shops are owned by Hindus who, although born and brought up in Las Palmas, have not lost their traditions or habits, which include the belief that should the first customer walk out empty-handed things will not go well all day. Many of them bless their establishment by sprinkling the entrance with holy water from the Ganges, witness **Perry's** in the Calle Luis Morote. On the third corner on the left in Ripoche is **Bazar Mavi,** excellent value for silk blouses and intricately crocheted tops. The tablecloths are also extremely good value. **Visanta**, a little further up on the left past the Levis shops, is one of the cheapest places for good quality cameras, watches, Ray-Ban sunglasses and electronic gear. Bargain hard.

Come out of Visanta and walk back down Ripoche in the direction of the Parque. This area of rundown shops and boarding houses is a favourite haunt of soldiers and sailors on leave from military service. Turn second left along **Secretario Artiles,** now occupied by stalls which were once on and around the Parque (it is advisable to keep out of shady side alleys). Down on your left, you have the novelty shop **Carrousel**, where you can buy a solar-powered toothbrush, china-soled socks which claim to stimulate your circulation, or tablets which when added to water turn into a complete set of cotton undies and a towel.

At the end of Secretario Artiles turn left into **Luis Morote**. Visit the **Perfumería Caribe** for a variety of duty-free perfumes – much cheaper than on the plane. This isn't the place for haggling but you may get little extras thrown in by appearing to be dubious! Although you are unlikely to be feeling the cold, why not prepare for harder times? Gran Canaria is one of the best places to buy leatherwear and fur coats, all of excellent quality and at superb prices. There is little demand among islanders – though on first nights of opera, you will see a great many furs around the Teatro Pérez Galdós – so most trade comes from holidaymakers. **Peletería Helena** (Luis Morote) offers high quality with coats and jackets made to measure. A little further up Luis Morote, still on the left-hand side, **M Nanwani** specialises in

Shoppers in Triana

arts and crafts from all parts of the world. For great gifts, try **Marfil Dani** on the other side of Luis Morote opposite **Zorba's** the disco. Lucky pyramids, children's watches, even football fans (of the ventilating type) are all found here. For more trinkets, drop in to **Napoleon**, not surprisingly beside the Hotel Concorde on Tomás Miller (first on your right off Luis Morote).

Although not typical of the Canary Islands, **Lladró** porcelain is much sought after and heavily taxed on the mainland. The shop which offers the best selection of Lladró is **Nara**, also good value for spirits and tobacco, on the corner of Tomás Miller and the beach. Opposite the shop, on the beachfront, is a great beach shop, **Praia do Rio**, which has the best in Brazilian beachwear at cheap prices. Next door (Alfredo L Jones, 42), **Dracena** the florist can prepare an arrangement of strelitzias and anthurums for you to take back home. Flowers are very good value in Gran Canaria so make the most of them. Further down Alfredo Jones (pronounced 'hoanies' by the locals), on the right hand side is **Electronica Bel**, purveyor of luxury sheets – even silk ones if you feel so inclined – Habana Club rum (not available everywhere) and good cigars. Still hankering after a tablecloth? Cross over to **Artesanía Paquita** where you can buy the real thing, which is Canary drawn-thread embroidery work, highly expensive, or a much cheaper Chinese replica. Again, try to bargain.

Lastly, hop in to either **Lurueña** or **Lopez** (one on each corner) for classic footwear and the latest fashions respectively.

If after all that shopping you only want a light lunch, try **La Cafetera** (back up Alfredo Jones, opposite the Reina Isabel Hotel); its crêpes and cakes are so delicious that you may end up eating more than you planned. Good value for money is **La Strada**, up Tomás Miller on the left-hand side (cross back over Luis Morote). It offers an excellent self-service buffet where you can eat as much as you like for relatively few pesetas.

Elegant shopping, traditional-style

The South

DAY 4

Sun, Sea and Sand

Southern Beaches

Once you've become familiar with your own stretch of coastline, then I suggest you try this full day sampling the idyllic coves of the coast west of Playa del Inglés, adjourning for a fish lunch en route. Take water or refreshment with you since most of these small beaches have no facilities to speak of.

–To starting point: Make your way to the GC*-1.–*

Follow the GC-1 until **Pasito Blanco**, a private marina which doesn't object to visitors during weekdays. On the hillside to the right, above the new campsite at Pasito Blanco, is the **Space Station**. Two bends on from here, take a dirt road off to the left (recognisable only by a dustbin which is there to collect rubbish from the ecologically-minded people who frequent this beach), which meanders down to a ramshackle hut surrounded by hen-coops and two or three stray dogs. Leave your car here; it is quite safe. Walk round the path to the left, over the rocks (easily followed), to **Montaña Arena**, a little-known beach frequented by locals. A

The South of Gran Canaria is a world apart. It caters for tourists who come in search of sun, sea, sand and organised entertainment, which is here aplenty. Remains of Guanches were found here during excavations for the new motorway, but they have been whisked out of public sight until the powers-that-be decide their fate. In the South, no-one in the tourist industry is interested in the past culture of the *Canarios*, not even the local press. The day itineraries on these pages can all be followed from southern resorts and will take you away from the crowded areas; the options highlight some of the best of the South's entertainments.

few ships ferrying contraband have run aground here but, providing you watch out for where the sand shelves away abruptly, the beach is safe.

Back in the car after your swim, continue down the coast to **Arguineguin**. Avert your eyes when you come to the unlovely cement factory, but stop off at the new complex which has recently been

built here to have a drink on one of the poolside verandahs. If you are hungry, try the restaurant **Hogar del Pescador**, the favourite haunt of models and photo crews who come to the south of the island for fashion shoots. It is extremely rustic and just round the corner from the cement factory, but its food is delicious, fresh and ridiculously cheap.

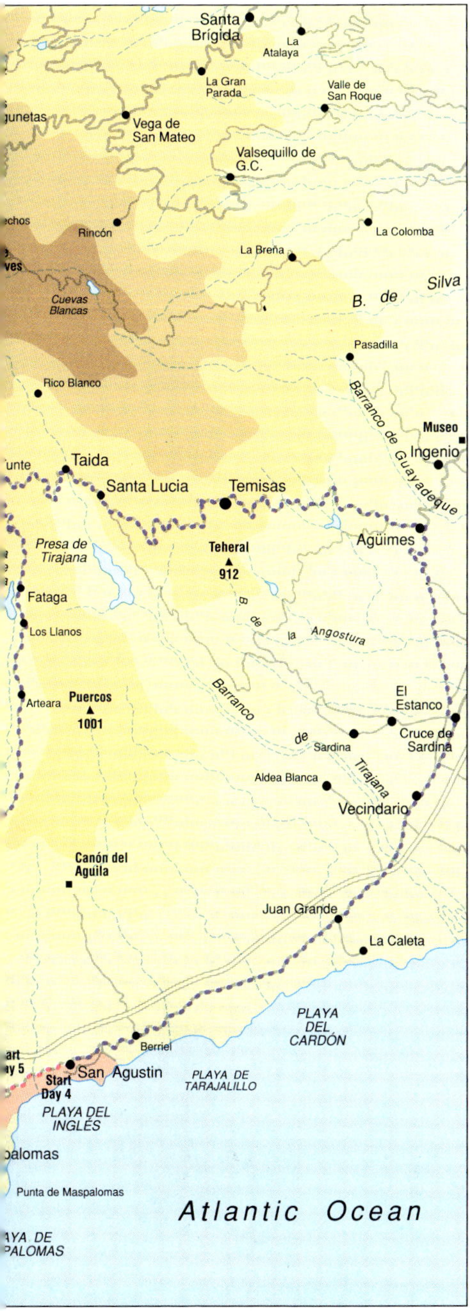

If you can manage without sustenance, drive through **Patalavaca** and past the multiple hotels whose rooms hang perilously over the sea. One of them, **Aquamarina**, is beautifully landscaped and its restaurant, Aquarela, is ideal for a romantic (but not inexpensive) night out. A little further on is **Los Caideros**, an enormous tourist complex built around a small and uninspiring beach, and beyond that **Puerto Rico**, which is tourism run amok. The best that can be said of Puerto Rico is that its beach is 'comfortable' for families with small children since it is too small for them to get lost. You can also water-ski, sail and hire paddle boats here.

Continue along the road and, if you feel in need of another dip, stop off at the **Barranco de Amadores** (Lovers' Gulley) but be warned: the walk down is not leisurely. Shortly before you come to Puerto de Mogán you will hit **Taurito**. The gigantic

Bathing belle, Puerto Rico

tourist complex that has been built around this small beach was so determined to make good use of the little space at its disposal that some of the hotel corridors are almost square up against the main road. The complex is unique of its kind, with a series of swimming pools in the style of Lago Martiánez in Puerto de la Cruz, Tenerife.

Further along, beyond a series of acute hairpin bends, is **Mogán**. The beach here is not impressive but the Venetian-style harbour area is very picturesque. Eat at the restaurant **Orilla del Mar** (no longer 'on the banks of the sea' as the name suggests), where fish is fresh and the salads are the best on the island (most of the avocados and papaws or papaya come from around here). Try papaw in Cointreau as a dessert – the fruit is reputed to have kept ex-President Reagan lively and, apart from that, is a good digestive. The waiter, who is also the owner, may even give you a song if the restaurant is not too busy.

Suitably refreshed, continue along the coast, taking in the unspoilt beach of **Veneguera**, further along the road on the left. Pass by **Tasarte** and **Tasartico**, up to **San Nicolás de Tolentino**, where you can visit the mini-zoo to see the eagle, and onto **La Aldea** (see *Calendar of Special Events*).

Again, there are two alternative routes here. You can either clamber over the rocks to the beach of La Aldea (only when the tide is not high) or, if you really want to be adventurous, hire a fishing boat and head for **Güigüi**, the most appealing beach on the island (appealing largely because of its inaccessibility). Fishermen are quite used to requests from tourists wanting to go to Güigüi and will wait to bring you back.

For your return journey it is just as well to take the same road, since to go by any other route entails at least another two hours' drive and dramatic changes in weather conditions. On the way back, take in **Las Meloneras**, just before Maspalomas with its famous miles of sand dunes, and have a *cubalibre* or *mojito* (rum with crushed lemon) in the bar/restaurant of Santiago before taking a final evening dip.

Waiting for a bite

For an excellent dinner with good service and better prices in a relaxed atmosphere, I suggest **Loopy's** in **San Agustín** where you can either try the closed pizzas – *calzone* – or the delicious and generous *pinchos* (kebabs) served Loopy-style. Dress up if you want to have a quick flutter at the casino in the **Hotel Tamarindos**. If you prefer something less risky, make for the **San Agustín Beach Club** where entertainment is guaranteed in relaxed and relaxing surroundings.

As you sit and reflect on the day and the miles of resorts you have passed, it is worth remembering that the whole coastline is a recent innovation; in 1963 a guide-book noted that Maspalomas was about to get itself a new town of hotels which will take away some of the wildness from this comparatively remote spot! It certainly has. Playa del Inglés alone has 350 restaurants and 50 hotels.

On the lonely strand at Güigüi

DAY 5

Inland

As a change from your resort, I recommend a scenic drive from Playa del Inglés up to the island's highest point, stopping for camel rides, swimming and lunch with views, and then down into almond country, from where there is a choice of two routes back. At the most, allow six hours.

–To starting point: drive along GC-1 until the junction where the restaurant Viuda de Franco stands on the right-hand side. Turn right for the road to Fataga. *See map on p. 50.**–*

Take a pullover and jeans to slip over your shorts/bikini/trunks. It's also a good idea to stock up on a hearty breakfast before tackling this trip. If you haven't had time beforehand, drop in to the **Viuda de Franco** and sample *un bocadillo de pata* (a roast ham sandwich) which should see you in good stead for the bends ahead. Follow the signposts for Fataga (not always as clear as they should be), basically bear straight ahead and then right. After the municipal rubbish dump the road is beautifully scenic, but it is also steep and narrow; watch out for oncoming *guaguas* (buses).

On one particularly dangerous bend in the road, you will see an open square with a little van selling everything from fruit to Mexican hats. The view from this lookout point is stunning so don't miss it – but be careful driving in and out.

In **Arteara**, drop in at the **Camel Safari Club** (again, a nasty entrance on the left). Here you can hire a camel for

Camel Safari

Into the hills at Tunte

Canary wrestling

half an hour for the modest price of around 1,000ptas per adult (children half-price). If you feel a little uncertain about this dubious pleasure (camels are rather uncomfortable mounts) you may prefer just to visit the stately animals – all 50 of them.

Back on the road, a little further on, you will see a signpost indicating **Las Lagunas** on the left. Follow this road to visit the **Posada Mirador** which offers some of the most breathtaking views of the island to be had from a hotel balcony. In view of the long, dry journey ahead, it's a good idea to take advantage of its pool. The restaurant is also tempting but save yourself for the Parador later; meanwhile have a quick drink and a snack and then get back on the road.

At **Tunte**, a beautiful unspoilt town, drive past the colourfully painted **Bar Guanche** and turn left for Tejeda. The road now becomes seriously serpentine with one bend on top of the other. Look down to your left to see the **Presa de Chira** (reservoir). Follow the signposts for **Los Pechos** which eventually take you up to the right. At 1,980m (6,496ft) this is the highest point on the island. Also known as **Pozo de las Nieves** (the Snow Well) because of a natural well within the military boundaries which is permanently ice-encrusted, this viewpoint affords wonderful photos of sunsets over Mount Teide on Tenerife. Note: fenced-off areas are out-of-bounds for military reasons.

Roques Bentaiga (right) and Nublo

Wind back down to the main road and turn up to the right for the **Parador**, lying just beyond nasty bends. Before lunch, drink an *aperitivo* on the terrace, which overlooks **Roque Nublo** and **El Fraile** (so-named because it looks like a friar kneeling at prayer). Try a Bitter Kas, which is similar to Campari but non-alcoholic, with *aceitunas en mojo* (olives in hot sauce). Lunch is served by cheerful waitresses dressed in traditional Canary costume. The *menú del día* always comprises typical Canary dishes and is excellent value for money.

Evening at Puerto de Mogán

After lunch, continue down to the village of **Tejeda** and follow the road past the **Roque Bentaiga** until you come to a crossroads at **El Montañón**. This is almond-tree country and all kinds of delicacies are offered at roadside stalls and shops, some of which have signs in English. Buy the delicious, sticky *bienmesabe* (literally 'I taste good'), made of honey, almonds and sugar and an excellent accompaniment to ice cream.

If you prefer an interesting, scenic run home with no great complications, take the road that runs through **Taidía**, **Santa Lucía** with its excellent craft shops, where **La Fortaleza**, a restaurant-cum-museum (open Monday–Saturday 9am–5pm), is well worth a visit, on through **Temisas** and down to **Agüimes**. If you have time, you could also take in the **Barranco de Guayadeque** (see *Pick and Mix, Option 2*). From **Agüimes**, town *par excellence* of the famous wrestlers of *lucha canaria* (something like Japan's sumo wrestling), make your way back via **Vecindario** to the main road and then back south.

More intrepid travellers whose vehicle is sufficiently sturdy should take the route past *las presas* (the dams). Rough terrain here is compensated for by spectacular scenery. This lonely route runs past three dams and alongside the beautiful **Pinar de Inagua** forest, regaining the beaten track at the village of **Mogán**.

Stop off at **Puerto de Mogán** to have something to eat and drink in the magnificent restaurant in the **Club del Mar** complex; a dip in the hotel's open-air Jacuzzi should leave you in fine fettle for the road back to your resort. Again, the drive requires caution: the point where the road offers the best views back over Mogán (especially when the sun is setting over the Puerto), lies on the worst bend on the island.

Option 5. Palmitos Park and Maspalomas

Camels, parrots, butterflies, golf and go-karts; the famous Maspalomas Dunes, amusements and shopping.

Los Palmitos Park (daily 9am–6pm) is a subtropical wildlife park up the road past El Tablero (there is a bus service). Its attractions include tropical birds and butterflies and gibbons – in particular an albino gibbon who was born on the premises. For a leisurely visit to the park you should allow two hours at least. Parrot shows are organised eight times daily. Although the park is a little cool first thing in the morning, it is also less busy then. At just under 1,000ptas for adults (half-price for children) it is good entertainment value. Ask for the guide to the local flora and look out for the cactus called 'mother-in-law's seat' (No 89).

Aquasur water-slide

On your way back down the road towards the sea, you will find **El Rancho Verde** on your right. Here you can hire a camel or a horse for a modest price and see the surrounding area from its back. If however the last thing you want to do is see more wildlife, then make your way a little farther down the road where, on the right, you can try your hand at go-kart racing (10am–11pm).

For something more refreshing, drop into **Aquasur**, the big

MIX

Prickly flowers

aquadrome just across the road from El Rancho Verde. Slide down the great multicoloured plastic tubes, fight against the waves in one of the swimming pools or merely lounge around.

Back in Maspalomas the **Maspalomas Golf Course** (18 holes), Avda Africa (Tel: 76 25 81), offers more sedate sport. Golf clubs can be hired.

For lunch in unforgettable surroundings, try the **Oasis Hotel** restaurant in Maspalomas (near the lighthouse). The buffet lunch is decently priced and the gardens with their peacocks and palm-trees are beautifully landscaped – perfect for an after-lunch snooze.

The Maspalomas sand dunes

For sunbathing, when there are no high winds, there is nowhere better than the **dunes** at Maspalomas. This is the nudist part of the beach but you can stick to your beachwear if you feel so inclined. If you want to experience nudism but feel shy, there are special stone rings which will shield you from unwelcome onlookers. Be warned: if there is a wind, towels etc quickly become buried, so keep a close eye on them if you go for a swim.

Ocean Park (10am–6pm) within the complex of Maspalomas Golf makes a refreshing change and you can bask in the shade if you feel so inclined. Grab an enormous rubber ring and float along.

Next door is **Holidayworld** (6pm–1am; closed Monday). For a little over 1,000ptas children and adults alike can brave the big dipper, the big wheel, the pirate ship, the fly-trap and many other white-knuckle rides. There is a good two hours' entertainment here if you like this kind of thing.

The most comprehensive shopping centre in the region of Playa del Inglés/Maspalomas is **Faro 2** (down Alpitours Street). The complex also comprises amusement parlours, a post-office, bureaux de change, newsagents and several good, well-priced restaurants (**Food Core 2** is exceptionally good value). People who just want to relax should head for **Mamas and Papas**, a piano bar which offers views over the dunes.

Option 6. Water Sports and Fishing Trips

Ride a sausage, water-ski, learn how to deep-sea dive or fish for a shark.

You will need to organise your day on the water with care. Spanish sailing laws oblige you to hire someone to pilot your boat as well as the boat itself, and although there are lots of people offering this service they don't always give value for money. Try at **Pasito Blanco** (ask at the petrol station or at the bar) to see if anyone will take you out, but make sure they are insured.

Galleon excursion

If this fails, the Pegasus Club (Tel: 15 10 00/73 63 33), beside the Aquamarina complex at **Patalavaca**, offers a day at sea (10am–5pm) with a barbeque lunch and German cakes and pastries in the late afternoon. A mini-bus is also laid on to take you to and fro (Tel: 15 10 00 or 73 63 33). The *Pegasus* is a beautiful sailing boat with

Lunch

a pleasant Viking-type skipper. The price of around 10,000ptas includes membership of the Pegasus club and discounts on future excursions.

If you prefer something more adventurous, try shark-fishing. The best place for chartering your own boat (six people minimum/eight maximum) is **Puerto Rico** round the far side of the marina. You take pot-luck here since they may be full (telephone bookings are not accepted) but they say that Tuesday and Friday are best. You can choose between two timetables: 9am–3.30pm or 3.30–8pm. If you want to fish it costs from 5,000ptas; if you only want to watch it costs a bit less.

If you don't mind an organised trip with more people, the *Punta Umbría II* at the entrance to the marina offers breakfast, lunch, shark-fishing, coffee and brandy, with a stop at a small cove along the way, for the modest price of around 3,500ptas (children under 10, half-price; Monday to Wednesday, Saturday, Sunday 11am–4.30pm). The return coach transfer from your resort is included in the price (Tel: 76 26 96).

The **Líneas Salmon** ferry runs between Puerto Rico, Mogán and Arguineguin almost every half hour. Mogán offers the possibility of a trip on the *Golden Submarine*, which starts from behind the **Club del Mar** complex. It's a good half-hour's fun for people who are not claustrophobic.

Those who prefer to keep their head above water can learn how to sail, windsurf, dive or water-ski at Puerto Rico. None of these activities can be learned quickly, however, and are not cheap. Pedal boats are far more economical, and the latest craze, the 'water-sausage', accommodating up to six people at a time, provides thrills at around 2,000ptas.

Good conditions

Shopping

There are lots of things to buy as souvenirs of Gran Canaria. Where you buy depends upon what you are after. Shops open at 10am (which is 11 on the mainland), close between 2pm and 4pm or 4.30pm, and close again around 8pm. Places such as **El Corte Inglés**, **Galerías Preciados** and **Zara**, all in the Mesa y López area, never close at lunchtime and others such as **Maya** (Triana) stay open all day around festivals such as Christmas and the 6th of January.

Not for taking home!

Items which are representative of Canary culture are found mainly between the **Calle Armas** in Vegueta (see *Day 1* in *Day Itineraries*) or in the **Fataga** shops, one of which is in the Pueblo Canario (see also *Day 1*) and the other in the Parque Santa Catalina next to the Tourist Information Bureau. The Calle Armas establishment is especially good for *naifes* (knifes with goathorn handles), which start off at around 6,000ptas. You can also buy *naife* brooches or even earrings. In wood, you can buy miniature replicas of *balcones canarios* (the famous wooden balconies), *arcones* (caskets), elaborately chiselled picture frames and *pilas*, tiny replicas of the filter stone traditionally used to collect water. The musical instruments on offer are *chacaras* (very big castanets), *timples* (very small guitars) and an odd collection of bones hung on goatskin (which works in a similar way to a washboard). In basketry, there are elaborate cane birdcages and typical local hats and baskets of all shapes and sizes. Earthenware includes the famous *ídolos de Tara*, *cachimbas* (clay pipes) and *pintaderas* (clay seals fashioned into brooches).

In the Fataga shops you will also find lace handkerchiefs, placemats and little figures dressed in the different native costumes of the different islands. Shop assistants will pack items so that they can be easily transported in suitcases.

Canary lace

If you want to buy Canary music, visit the music department in the Corte Inglés (Mesa y López). If it is classical music that you want, buy the *Cantos Canarios* by Teobaldo Power or anything by the modern composer Falcón Sanabria. For folk music, the best shops are **Los Sabandeños, Mestisay** or **Los Gofiones**. In more modern music, the **Parranda Cuasquías** and **Los Coquillos** will demonstrate that there is more to Spanish music than Julio Iglesias.

The Mesa y López area is particularly good for clothes, with shops such as **Cortefiel**, **Selección 7**, **Prenatal** (for children's clothes) and **Zara** offering a wide range of possibilities to suit all pockets. Shoe shops abound. You will find **Lurueña** and **López** again but also **Don Juan** at the bottom end of the street.

For anything in the way of cameras, computer games etc try **Maya** in Triana, which, unlike the other Indian shops where the custom is to haggle, offers reasonable prices with a guarantee. For souvenirs, look out for the gold *pintaderas* or the little gold replicas of Gran Canaria.

Canary tobacco is another popular purchase. Apart from the cigars, either in stacks from **La Palma** or in boxes (**Condal**), both of which can be purchased in the **Canteras** shops or in the Corte Inglés, the most popular strong tobacco is **Coronas,** but the strongest of the strong is **Kruger** or **Mecánicos**, both of which come without filters and are rough.

Local flowers

For wine, try the malmseys from Lanzarote. **El Grifo is** the best white wine and **Malvasía** the best rosé. As a rule, red wines are not recommended: *Vino del Monte*, which you can buy in local bars the Tafira and La Atalaya areas, is an acquired taste!

If you liked it when you tried it, take home some *gofio* and *turrón*, also on sale in all the supermarkets. Finally, buy a bouquet of strelitzias to brighten your first days back home or some *drago* seeds to grow your own magic dragon-tree back home.

Eating

Gran Canaria is very cosmopolitan and many restaurants offer international cuisine, which often means prawn cocktail, steak and Black Forest gâteau. I have not recommended any of these venues since they are the easiest for visitors to find.

The Canary Islands have a cuisine all of their own. It makes full use of the vegetables which are produced here in abundance and the fish which are so readily available. Local chefs can also do wonderful meat dishes, though meat is usually imported and vacuum-packed. However, goat meat and rabbit – try the succulent *conejo al salmorejo* (rabbit in hot chilli sauce) – are local and fresh. Specialities of the region are the *potaje de berros* (water-cress soup) with *gofio* (toasted cornflour), *caldo de pescado* (fish and vegetables with a coriander sauce and *gofio*) and *sancocho* (salt fish with normal potatoes and sweet potatoes).

Be sure to try the local fish: *cherne* (a kind of bass), *sama*, a type of seabream and *viejas* (not unlike parrotfish), all with *mojo verde*, a herby garlic sauce. The cheeses of the region are also

Special today

Basic ingredients

magnificent: *queso flor* from Gran Canaria is mild, but if you like strong cheese try the *majorero* (from Fuerteventura). Accompany fish or cheese with the famous *papas arrugadas* (small salty jacket potatoes) with *mojo picón* (hot chilli sauce).

Vegetarians are well catered for. *Ropa vieja* (literally 'old clothes') is chick-peas with diced potatoes and other vegetables (though be careful since meat is sometimes slipped in too). *Moros y cristianos* (literally, Moors and Christians) is white rice with kidney beans. Salads make full use of fruits: for example, *aguacate* (avocado) and melon are mixed together with papaw and strawberries.

If you have a sweet tooth, try the *bienmesabe* (a honey and almond confection) and the *turrón* (a kind of nougat).

Eating out is cheap. As with most things, the south is more expensive, given the competition. In the following list $ indicates a meal for less than 3,000ptas for two, everything included; $$ is under 8,000ptas; and $$$ means under 15,000ptas.

Canary cuisine

CA'CHO DAMIAN
León y Castillo, 26, Las Palmas
Tel: 365323
Choose from a tempting array of enormous bowls on the counter or opt for the set menu. Allow staff to advise you on wine.
($$) Visa

EL HERREÑO
Mendizabal, 5-7, Las Palmas
Tel: 310513
The set menu is usually tempting but if not try a mixture of dishes in *raciones*. Try the *churros de pescado* (fish in batter) and the *carajaca* (liver). Ask for wine from El Hierro: the rosé is the best (*rosado*).
($) No credit cards

TENDERETE
León y Castillo, 91, Las Palmas
Tel: 246957
The best place for Canary food, but prices match quality. This is where

Fresh fish

Juan Carlos eats when he's in town. Follow the recommendations of the owner.
($$$) Visa

Las Grutas de Artiles
Las Meleguinas s/n, Santa Brígida (Centre)
Tel: 640575
Built inside caves, the setting is impressive. Good food, typically Spanish with a touch of the Canary Islands.
($$) Visa, Master Card

Tenderete II
Av S B de Tirajana, Edificio Aloe, Playa del Inglés
Tel: 761460
Nice atmosphere, great food and very good service.
($$) All credit cards accepted

Spanish Food (Regional)

Amaiur
Pérez Galdós, 2, Las Palmas
Tel: 370717
Basque.
Excellent imaginative dishes from one of the greatest gastronomic regions of Spain. Expect to rub shoulders with the local politicians since it lies across the road from the Government offices in San Bernardo.
($$$) American Express, Diners, Master Card, Visa

El Padrino
J.Nazareno, 1, Las Coloradas
Las Palmas
Tel: 272094
Seafood.
Good fresh fish served in pleasant out-of-town surroundings with fine views over Las Canteras. Try *parrillada de pescado*, an enormous dish of grilled fish of all varieties, washed down with the white wine El Grifo from Lanzarote (*semiseco* – medium dry).
($$) All credit cards accepted

El Yantar
Av Mesa y López, 43, Las Palmas
Basque/Spanish.
This is the place for mouth-watering

Cave restaurant, Barranco de Guayadeque

Buffet spread

suckling pig or leg of lamb. Excellent wines: try the Añares by Rioja. Good service.
($$) Visa

El Secuestro
Teror (centre)
Grilled meat, succulent *chorizo* and black puddings (*morcillas*) from Teror. Not for those with little appetite. The atmosphere is highly rustic and the place is always crowded on Sunday and holidays. Do not fill up on the delicious hot bread and garlic butter that arrives before your main meal. The house red wine is nice but drivers should be warned that it is also potent.
($) Closed Monday. No credit cards

L'Orangerie
Av del Oasis s/n
Hotel Maspalomas Palm Beach (South)
Tel: 762924
The menu changes every day according to what is in season in the fields and seas. Elegant restaurant serving excellent food.
($$$) All credit cards accepted

Rias Bajas
Edificio Playa Sol, Av de Tirajana, Playa del Inglés
Tel: 764033
This restaurant specialises in Galician cuisine, so seafood is a must. Try the *empanada* (a kind of vegetable and tuna pie) and the *tarta de Santiago* (almond cake). Be guided by the chef.
($$) Visa, American Express

Others

La Pasta Real
Secretario Padilla, 28, Las Palmas
Tel: 262267
Italian and macrobiotic.
Small restaurant with the best food in town, despite the less appealing setting. The owner used to work in the Scottish town of St Andrew's and therefore speaks fluent English with a broad Scots accent. Service is excellent. The *spaghetti a la carbonara* is always worth a try. The menu, chalked up on a blackboard, includes so many delicious dishes you will probably want to return.
($) Visa, Diners

Le Français
Sargento Llagas, 18, Las Palmas
Tel: 266762
Wonderful food from the great gastronomic regions of France. The desserts in particular are mouthwatering. This is a small restaurant with excellent service.
($$) Visa, American Express

Seafood paella

Night

Possibly one of the reasons for the Canary Islander's famous *aplatanamiento* (literally the 'state of becoming a banana') is that they love to stay out until all hours, dancing and making merry. If you decide to drop in on any of the special events, you will see how people go all out to have a good time even in the smallest village. Of course, the bigger the festivity, the more elaborate the celebration, but you can always count on *papagüevos* (giants on stilts or enormous-headed dwarves), fireworks and a *verbena*, a shindig in the village square with rollicking live music supplied by the local band. (Look out for the old faithfuls of the popular Banda de Agaete, an essential ingredient in any good celebration.)

The best thing about these celebrations is their community spirit. Apart from the very few slow dances, everyone dances with everyone else. People usually drink beer or *cubalibre* and no celebration is complete without the *tollos* and *pejines* (two kinds

life

Glitz at Pachá

of salty fish with a texture like chewing-gum, guaranteed to give you a healthy thirst). This and Carnival are the only occasions when you are expected to pay as you drink. Note: a waist-pouch is wise since handbags are cumbersome and wallets in danger.

If you are looking for something more sophisticated in nightlife, then Gran Canaria is the place for you also. Be warned on two counts: nobody who is anybody goes out before midnight and discos exist primarily for facilitating brief encounters with the opposite sex. The locals are not backward at coming forward and like to practise their language skills – especially since the level of decibels in the disco usually makes close proximity essential.

As with shops (see *Shopping*), different areas offer different kinds of nightlife. Towards Vegueta and behind Triana bars are more restrained in style, designed for the 'older' young generation. This is totally in keeping with the atmosphere of this area: more relaxed and refined. Of these, **Pool** in the Calle San Pedro behind the theatre offers live music, a pool (as the name indicates) and pleasant company. **Yurfa** is another old favourite. Housed in an old Canary building in the Calle Perdomo, this bar offers good music, art exhibitions, excellent prices and lots of corners where you can sit down and talk without straining the vocal chords. Take a taxi to the theatre around 11pm and work your way round.

After midnight, the place to go is the Plaza de la Victoria.

Bar Heineken

Again, take a taxi. The neighbours who live above the bustling noisy pubs don't take kindly to revellers so stand under the protection of the awnings: more than one has been known to 'water' the clientele. **Heineken** is the most popular of these tiny bars. The jukebox music is mainly golden oldies!

Alternatively, ask the taxi driver to take you to the Calle Isla de Cuba. The new bar on the corner, **La Pila,** is currently the most popular, and right next door is an old favourite, **La Tienda**. Cheap and cheerful, this is frequented by the less pretentious Canary youth.

Around 2am, you should be thinking of making a move towards El Puerto, which you can walk to from Calle Isla de Cuba. If you are looking for glitz and glitter, then **Pachá**, behind the Saba car park and down on the harbour front, is the place to go. You can squeeze onto the tiny dance floor in front of a giant video screen, or have a relatively quiet drink on the outside terrace.

If you are looking for something a little more informal in the jeans line, **Toca-Toca** in the Secretario Artiles is extremely lively at weekends as is its neighbour, **Area,** a disco/bar where they play only Spanish music. The perennially popular **Diseño** in Nicolás Estévanez and **Utopía** in Tomás Miller have maintained their appeal over the years by constantly revising their image. Both are very loud and crowded.

If your tastes in music and nightlife are more sedate, try the piano-bar **La Clave,** in Alfredo Jones, which allows singalongs. And if you want to try your hand (and feet) at dancing *sevillanas* and flamenco, try the **Sala Rociero** in the Calle Olof Palme, just round the corner from the Plaza de la Victoria.

For those with stamina, **Cuperón** opens when all the other bars close (at 6am) and offers good music through until midday.

Down South, where you go depends on which resort you are staying in but, generally speaking, each shopping centre has one or two places which are the in-places for that area. These change from one year to the next so you must play it by ear – literally. Recently, however, the Kasbah's biggest pulls are **Garage** and **Fantasy Island** whilst in the Plaza shopping centre in Maspalomas it is **Pachá** and **Chic.**

Hot but cool

Calendar of Special Events

It is hardly an exaggeration to say that every day is a *fiesta* in Gran Canaria. Celebration of name days, religious feast days, local historical events and ancient traditions are frequent. Rare is the day when fireworks are not going off somewhere round the island. Like everything else in Gran Canaria, the local festivities are a peculiar mixture of pagan revelry and Christian solemnity.

If the celebration is common to the whole of the island there may be organised competitions of *lucha canaria* or even exhibitions of local dancing and singing.

JANUARY

New Year is a major event. People elebrate either at home, on the beach vith fireworks or in a nightclub or lisco where *collones* (special festiviies complete with party hats, streamrs and silly plastic noses) are organsed. Whichever way, tradition insists hat revellers swallow 12 grapes, hime by chime, for good luck, plus ots of *cava* (sparkling wine).

On the 5th islanders buy presents or **Día de Reyes** (the Day of the Three Wise Men) which falls on the 5th. On the evening of the 5th every illage and town holds a procession of the Three Wise Men. As the processions are held at different times, it

Fiesta dress

is possible to see up to nine Wise Men on a variety of mounts (camels, donkeys or horses) or even motorised. The 6th is a national holiday though restaurants stay open.

FEBRUARY

The main celebration is **Carnival**, usually the last week of February and the first week of March, though different parts of the island begin and end at different times, beginning in Agüimes and ending in Maspalomas. Look out for the competition of the **Murgas**, bands of singers who poke fun at local politicians and events; the **Elección de la Reina**, the Carnival Queen contest awash in sequins and feathers; the **Fiesta de la Sábana**, the Sheet Party, where all you need is a sheet and imagination; the different *mogollones*, open air dances with *salsa* music; the Carnival Parade and the **Entierro de la Sardina**, the Burial of the Sardine followed by the Widows' Dance, possibly the best part of the whole Carnival.

MARCH/APRIL

After a month of pagan revelry, 19 March is the Feast of **San José** (St Joseph, and thus Father's Day). Since the Spaniards celebrate their name day, this is one of the most important days of the year.

Semana Santa (the dates change every year), most famous for the celebrations at Seville, is also taken very seriously in Gran Canaria, with everything closed on Holy Thursday and Good Friday. Processions abound in all parts of Gran Canaria. 29 April marks the controversial celebration of the Spanish **Conquest.**

MAY

1 May is Labour Day (**Día del Trabajo**) with the traditional demonstrations of the trade unions. The 30th is the **Día de Canarias**, an official holiday celebrated throughout the Canary Islands to mark the anniversary of the granting of autonomous rule to the archipelago.

Carnival revellers

JUNE

17 June is the feast day of **Corpus Christi** when streets of various towns and Vegueta in Las Palmas are painstakingly covered with carpets of flowers. The 24th marks the feast of **San Juan**, doubly important since it is also the anniversary of the founding of the city of Las Palmas. A whole week of events is organised, including open-air concerts and folklore. On the night of San Juan, which is the Spaniards' equivalent of Hallowe'en, bonfires are built, especially on the beaches.

JULY

The 16th marks the celebrations of the **Fiestas del Carmen**, patron saint of all those who work on the seas and greatly revered by the Canary islanders. The most moving processions are held in the Puerto de la Luz, La Isleta, Gáldar and Mogán. From the 22–25 July, the most important celebrations for Gáldar and San Bartolomé de Tirajana take place, the **Fiestas de Santiago el Apóstol**.

AUGUST

The other great traditional pagan celebration is held on 4 August: **La Bajada de la Rama** in Agaete. This celebrates one of the rain-making rituals of the *Canarios*. The 29th is the celebration of the **Virgen de la Cuevita** in Artenara, a torchlit night procession.

SEPTEMBER

Possibly the biggest celebration on Gran Canaria is held on 8 September, the **Virgen del Pino** in Teror. The locals make a night pilgrimage to Teror, some of them on their knees. The

Religious procession

10th marks another typical *Canarios'* celebration, the **Fiesta del Charco** in San Nicolás de Tolentino where the locals fish with their hands in a specially rigged pool.

OCTOBER

The **Fiestas de la Naval** are celebrated in La Isleta and the area called La Naval, around 6 October. They celebrate the victory over Sir Francis Drake in 1595. National festivities, consisting mainly of military parades, of the **Día de la Hispanidad** take place on the 12th.

NOVEMBER/DECEMBER

1 November is **Día de los Difuntos** (All Souls' Day). 6 December is the **Día de la Constitución** (to celebrate the Constitution on which democratic Spain is based), not usually an official holiday. The 25th, of course, is **Christmas** when you should look out for the *belenes* (nativities) in San Gregorio, Telde, in the Museo de Piedras, Ingenio and the 'live' nativity in Agaete.

Practical Information

Inter-island transport

GETTING THERE

The usual way to reach Gran Canaria is by plane – though you can always opt for the combination of flying to Tenerife, to the Reina Sofía airport and then taking a taxi up to Santa Cruz where you can catch the Jetfoil, a kind of hovercraft, directly to Las Palmas de Gran Canaria. The Jetfoil service runs a winter and a summer timetable. To find out when there is a jetfoil available (the travelling time is 1hour and 40 minutes), phone Trasmediterránea, Tel: (928) 265650. There are lots of charter flights to Gran Canaria. Although it is possible to find flight only deals, it usually works out cheaper to take something with accommodation already included.

The airport at Gandó in Gran Canaria is in the process of being extended to accommodate not only tourists to this island but also those travelling on to Lanzarote or Fuerteventura. If you are travelling under your own steam, you can either take the airport bus to the centre of Las Palmas de Gran Canaria (around 500ptas) or catch a taxi, which will charge a standard price of around 2,000ptas. To travel down south if you are not on a package trip is expensive. Although a regular bus service does exist, it leaves from the far side of the very busy motorway – not the airport itself – and there is no bridge to help you get across. Taxis charge 4,000–5,000ptas for the run to Playa del Inglés. If you are going further than that, ask for a quote first.

TRAVEL ESSENTIALS

When to Go

High season (*temporada alta*) begins in October and runs through to April/May. Although it is true to say that Gran Canaria has sun and even temperatures all year round, the best months are September and October, when schools restart in Spain. The south enjoys sunshine all year round, which is why many tour operators have introduced sunshine guarantee clauses in their holiday offers. However, although the weather is beautifully warm

Year-round sun

in January and February, the water itself is icy cold.

July and August are months to be avoided if possible since this is when the locals are on holiday themselves and everything is much more crowded. It is also when Las Palmas de Gran Canaria is victim of the *panza de burro* (see *Climate*) which produces intense heat but little sunshine.

Climate

The average temperature in Gran Canaria is 22°C (72°F) although as I point out throughout this guidebook the temperature varies according to the altitude. The south in general is rarely overcast, though on the days when there is *viento del sur*, a kind of sirocco, the sky is a dull grey. It is a mistake to think you are quite safe from sunburn on these days, for the ultra-violet rays are trapped between the leaden sky and the beach, producing what the locals call *resol*, 'double sun'.

When the day is windy, the locals avoid the Playa del Inglés and Maspalomas and make for beaches further west, such as Puerto Rico and Taurito, which are sheltered.

In Las Palmas de Gran Canaria, the *sirocco* brings sand from Morocco, producing a very disagreeable thunderous atmosphere (*polvo en suspensión* – literally 'dust in the air'). People who suffer from allergies should try to head south when this occurs since to stay in the city until the rain rinses away the problem can mean a great deal of suffering. When it rains, it rains hard, but only in very short bursts and the temperature remains the same. March and April are the months when the weather is most unsettled, but even then this affects only the higher regions of the island.

ar-round swimming

Two other phenomena which you should be aware of are the famous *panza de burro* or 'donkey's belly', an enormous grey cloud which settles over the capital of the island in July/August, producing intense heat, and the *mar de nubes* (or 'sea of clouds'). You can climb up above the clouds but any hopes of taking panoramic photographs of the island are ruined. However, neither of these phenomena tend to last more than one day at a time. Rolling mists (and they travel at speed) can also be found on higher ground.

Clothing

Coats and jackets are not needed but a light cardigan or pullover is necessary if you are intending to travel up to higher regions. Sunglasses are a must and a pair of plastic sandals for use on some of the beaches is a good idea since there may be rocks underfoot.

Sensible footwear is necessary if you are thinking of walking around to any great extent and some kind of head protection is also important. Men should pack a tie if they intend visiting the casino. Umbrellas are not necessary; in the rare case of needing one, you will find that they are dirt cheap in the Corte Inglés in Las Palmas.

Documents

You need a valid passport and an international driving licence. You should also take out some kind of travel insurance to safeguard against accidents and pick up the E111 form from your local post office before leaving home; this entitles EC citizens to free medical treatment.

A religious mix

about visitors confusing them with the Balearic Islands or with Tenerife.

Electricity

The electricity supply is 220 volts, and the Spaniards use round two-pin sockets, so UK visitors will need an adaptor for any electrical appliances. Four-star and five-star hotels provide hairdriers. Laundry services are cheap and often preferable to the results of a travel iron.

Time Differences

There is an hour's difference between mainland Spain and the Canary Islands. Gran Canaria is usually on the same time as Great Britain but when the clocks change there may be a week or so when there are two hours' difference.

GETTING ACQUAINTED

Geography

The Canary archipelago is on latitude 28° and comprises seven inhabited islands, an eighth which is partially inhabited (La Graciosa), four or five uninhabited islands (Lobos, Montaña Clara, Alegranza, Roque del Este, Roque del Oeste) and another mythical island, San Borondón (St Brendan's), which appears and disappears at will.

The seven islands are divided between two provinces: Las Palmas which includes Gran Canaria, Fuerteventura, Lanzarote, La Graciosa (and the uninhabited islands) and Tenerife which takes in Tenerife, La Palma, El Hierro and La Gomera.

People in Gran Canaria are very touchy about visitors confusing them with the Balearic Islands or with Tenerife.

Government and Economy

The Canary Islands have an autonomous regional government with fully devolved powers in very limited fields. The economy, which was formerly dependent upon agriculture, began to rely heavily on tourism in the 1960s. This industry now represents almost 80 percent of the archipelago's total income.

At times, the Canary islanders have protested that the central government in Spain is insensitive to their situation as isolated islands. Since most products are imported, the cost of living is high compared with the rest of Spain. With full integration of Spain and the Canary Islands in the EC, locals believe that their cost of living could suffer.

Parties of a nationalist nature have sprung up over the last few years. One of these in particular, ATI, has had so much success that it holds the balance of power in a regional coalition government with the Socialist party, PSOE.

Population and Religion

There is a great ethnic mix in Gran Canaria. People from all parts of the world have come here for business or pleasure and stayed to become fully integrated in society. Thus all religions have been represented here for some time. The Templo Ecuménico in the south holds multilingual religious ceremonies. There is also a mosque in the Yumbo shopping centre in the south and various churches of the Latter-Day Saints scattered over the island.

MONEY MATTERS

It is best to come with peseta traveller's cheques and local currency. Money changers are many and their rates differ widely. Avoid bureaux de change in hotels if possible. Always try to change money in banks, open from 9am–2pm but not on Saturday.

Some banks have currency exchange points (eg Caja de Madrid in Calle Albareda) like cash machines outside their premises. These are not recommended unless in case of emergency.

Credit cards are widely accepted, above all American Express and Visa. Cash points in the area of El Puerto are usually housed inside booths, for obvious reasons, and allow you to carry out your transactions in the language of your choice.

Remember that the harbour area suffers from all the typical problems of such a district, so do not display money or carry wallets in back pockets. A money belt or a pouch are wise investments.

Tipping

Perhaps expected in restaurants and hairdressers but not elsewhere. Ten percent is the norm.

GETTING AROUND

Las Palmas de Gran Canaria with over 350,000 inhabitants is almost worse to drive in than London. People use their cars for absolutely everything and want to park right next to their destination. Since the city was originally planned for a small number of vehicles and it is estimated that there is an average of at least two cars per person of driving age in the capital, the effect is bedlam. For inner-city travel I suggest you use the *guaguas* (buses), which are cheap (75ptas) and cheerful. A *bono guagua* (pronounced boneoh wawa) which can be used for 10 journeys costs 500ptas and can be bought in any bank.

Taxis are good value with the longest run in the city costing around 300ptas. Walking is only pleasant in Las Palmas in pedestrian areas such as Vegueta, the Avda Marítima or around Las Canteras.

To travel around the island you can use the green buses, the SALCAI (Tel: 36 88 31 for information), which run a particularly fast line down to the south, or the UTINSA (Tel: 37 36 25) which tend to be slower and serve rural areas. Both leave from the bus station across from the Parque San Telmo.

However, the easiest way to travel round the island is by car, especially since the introduction of colourful new sign-posting. You can hire anything from a Seat Panda (approximately 2,000ptas per day) to a Mitsubishi mini-van which costs around 10,000ptas a day and seats nine. Rates are much the same at all companies, but Avis, Betacar and Autos Moreno offer the most reliable service. There is a larger variety of vehicles to choose from outside the airport.

For organised excursions, Tamaragua (Tel: 27 20 00) in Nicolás Estévanez and in the south, or any of the branches of Ultramar Express (Tel: 27 30 22) offer you everything from shark-fishing to belly-dancing at competitive prices.

To travel between the islands, the Jetfoil serves Fuerteventura and Tenerife (Tel: 26 56 50) and ferries which take cars serve all the islands. There is an excellent inter-island flight service (Tel: 57 42 20/25 41 40 for information), but remember that flights are heavily booked at Christmas, Easter and in July/August. Book in any travel agency.

Winding roads

Idyllic anchorage

HOURS & HOLIDAYS

The people in the Canary Islands work according to two timetables: one for the so-called summer and the other for the rest of the year. Most of the time, life is geared to schedules on mainland Spain. Schools start at 8–8.30am (take note if your hotel/apartment is near a school), but there are so many children of school age (although the birthrate in the Canary Islands has fallen) that high school students are taught in shifts and may still be at their desks at 8pm.

Offices are supposed to open at about 9am but few make it before 9.30, apart from the banks, some of which begin at 8.30am. Shops open around 10am, which is the time El Corte Inglés opens, although food shops are open earlier. They close again at 2pm and reopen around 4pm. Everything closes around 8pm though you will find places in Las Canteras which stay open later.

The summer timetable is applied by offices such as the Tourist Information Office, in the months of July and August, due to lack of staff. In those months offices open from 9am–2pm and do not reopen in the afternoon.

People in Gran Canaria do not take a *siesta*. In fact, they do not appear to sleep very much at all, which possibly explains the slow rhythm all through the day. Nightlife rarely begins until around midnight and continues on well into the morning.

Taxis are available 24 hours a day and the airport is also open all night.

Remember that public holidays (see *Calendar of Special Events*) are kept religiously – only restaurants and some bars do not close. If the holiday falls on a Thursday, Friday is also taken as a holiday. People all over Spain are experts at inventing *puentes*, ie long weekends.

ACCOMMODATION

Generally speaking, the accommodation in the south of the island is of excellent standard and offers possibilities for all pockets. Las Palmas de Gran Canaria tends to cater more for business people than for tourists *per se* and accommodation divides between the very good and the very bad with little in between. Since people no longer tend to stay the whole time in Las Palmas but go south for the sunshine, lots of the hotels have become rather rundown.

In the capital, the best hotels cost around 12,000ptas per night whilst more modest, yet decent accommodation costs around 4,000ptas per night. In the following recommendations *$* indicates accommodation under 5,000 ptas, *$$* is under 20,000ptas, and *$$$* over 20,000ptas. All price guides are for a double room.

Hotel Santa Catalina (Tel: 243040, *$$$*) is possibly the most expensive of the hotels in Las Palmas, clocking in at around 20,000ptas per night, but worth it. On **Las Canteras** itself, however, there is a wide choice to suit all tastes. **Hotel Imperial Playa** (Tel: 264854, *$$*) which belongs to the NH chain is, like most, a refurbished old hotel with wonderful views and magnificent rooms. **Hotel Meliá** (Tel: 267600, *$$*), **Reina Isabel** (Tel: 260100, *$$*) and the **Hotel Sansofé** (Tel: 224062, *$$*) are also on the beachfront. Hotel Sansofé should be given a miss if it only has back rooms available since the hotel borders on the seedier side of Las Canteras and the back streets are active, in all senses.

Should you want something cheaper and yet still decent, try **Hotel Cantur**

(Tel: 262304, $) a little back from the beachfront but still on Las Canteras or **Hotel Atlanta** (Tel: 265062, $) behind the Reina Isabel in Calle Alfredo Jones. Clocking in at the same price, and possibly the best bet if you want to do your own thing, are the apartments **Colón Playa** (Tel: 265954, $) on the beachfront at the end of Alfredo Jones, which offer seaviews and a central position.

Down south, you can choose between different resorts and different types of accommodation. In San Agustín, favoured by islanders, **Hotel Gloria Palace** (Tel: 768300, $$), built largely for congresses, is new, well-laid out and exceptionally comfortable. In Playa del Inglés, **Hotel Parque Tropical** (Tel: 760712, $$) is beautifully designed, central and decently priced as well as being the place where local and international stars stay when appearing at the nightclub Don Gato next door.

The hotel if you are staying in Maspalomas is the **Oasis**, with double rooms either looking onto the Oasis or onto the sea. Either way is beautiful and costs around 20,000ptas for a double. Patalavaca, just round the corner from Arguineguín, offers the **Steigenberg Canaria** (Tel: 150400, $$) with incredible sunset vistas. In Mogán, (Tel: 740100, $$) the beautiful **Club de Mar** complex (little Venice) costs a very decent 10,000ptas.

However, as I said, you can find apartments and bungalows to suit all pockets. Consult the travel agencies mentioned in *Getting Around* or in El Corte Inglés.

Camping is another option, but sites tend to be noisy (everybody takes their TV!), crowded and with few facilities. They are good for meeting people, however, and for travellers on shoestring budgets. (Information from the campsites at Pasito Blanco and Taurito.)

CULTURAL EVENTS

The Canary islanders have always felt culturally disadvantaged compared with their fellow countrymen, though very unnecessarily so. Consequently a great deal of effort is made to compensate. An esteemed International Festival of Classical Music is held every February (tickets and programmes from SOCAEM well in advance to avoid disappointment; Tel: 291944/292588). There are also festivals of opera, light opera (*zarzuela*) – details from SOCAEM also – and ballet, and travelling theatre groups regularly appear at the Teatro Pérez Galdós. The University of Las Palmas de Gran Canaria organises various courses throughout the year (see newspapers for details) and a summer school every August, with speakers from all parts of the world. The CAAM also organises excellent seminars to coincide with their exhibitions.

HEALTH & EMERGENCIES

Should you need attention for anything more serious than insect bites, sunburn or a gippy stomach, you should make for the emergency services (*Urgencias*) in any of the following hospitals: Clínica del Pino in the Calle Tomás Morales (Tel: 23 11 99), the Materno-Infantil (principally maternity and children's hospital but attends all kinds of cases and ages), Avda Marítima del Sur (Tel: 32 03 33) or the Hospital Insular, also in the Avda Marítima (Tel: 31 30 33), in Las Palmas de Gran Canaria. These are the hospitals which look after the general population. There are usually English-speaking doctors and nurses around, but if you need to explain your problem without misunderstanding of any kind, then your best bet is to make for the Hospital Inglés, Paseo de la Cornisa,1 (Tel: 25 42 43) which, as its name indicates, has English-speaking staff.

Do not drink the water from the tap under any circumstances. Try to avoid it even for brushing your teeth and eschew ice in your drinks. Bottled water comes in two types, *con* (with) or *sin* (without) *gas*, so you do not have to drink the 'bubbly' if you don't want to. Buy this in supermarkets as bars inflate prices. Should you be caught by a dose of diarrhoea, ask for Fortasec in the chemist's and avoid drinking alcohol for at least six hours. One tablet does the trick.

Although it is immensely difficult, try to avoid over-exposure to the sun. Keep out of direct sunlight from 1–4pm and watch out for kids catching double dosage in the water. Acute sunburn or sunstroke should be treated in a hospital (Clínica Scandinavica (Tel: 771638) or the Suomi British Clinic (Tel: 762742) both in the south).

Crime

The people of Gran Canaria are still peaceful and law-abiding but, as happens in any big city with a busy harbour area, there are problems, especially bag-snatching and theft. Do not court trouble and only carry your passport and other papers around when absolutely necessary, ie when changing money. The area beyond and behind the Sansofé hotel is not particularly safe at night and is perfectly easy to avoid. The same can be said of Ripoche.

The south is not free from these problems either, especially its bungalows, which are less well protected. Should you have problems contact the nearest *comisaría* (police station). Sometimes, you may need to ask your consulate for help, since not all police stations have interpreting services or police who can speak languages other than Spanish. For emergencies of any kind, dial 091.

Typical tiling

SPORT

The south of the island is the place for water sports, with lessons in water-skiing, deep-sea diving, underwater fishing, windsurfing and sailing all on offer for those who have time to learn. The best place for these, and for shark fishing, is Puerto Rico.

If you want to go your own way without tuition then Pozo Izquierdo is the best place for windsurfing (signposted on the road down to the south, around Arinaga). The world championship heats were held here only recently. Playa del Aguila, just before San Agustín and Bahía Feliz are also good for windsurfing. For ordinary surfers, the area around Bañaderos and the end of the Canteras beach, beside the road out to the north, are the best places.

Vela latina (a highly skilful type of sailing) is not easy to understand but very popular with the natives (the sport generates a lot of betting). *Lucha canaria* may be programmed to celebrate special events and is very exciting to watch – as are the *lucha del garrote* (*juego del garrote*) competitions.

There is a golf course at Maspalomas (see *Pick and Mix Option 5*) and Bandama (see *Day 3*). The football season begins in September – but visiting spectators should avoid matches between U D Las Palmas and Tenerife, which are well known for their violence.

MAPS

Pick up the excellent freebies in El Corte Inglés in Las Palmas. The Tourist Information office (Parque Santa Catalina) can also provide you with detailed maps.

TOILETS

Unlike on mainland Spain, toilets are generally well-tended. Don't use the toilets in the Parque Santa Catalina, however, or any other public toilet. Agaete doesn't win the award for Gran Canaria's most scrupulous town on this account.

Lack of toilets is a handicap of Carnival merrymaking. Portable loos are grossly insufficient. Your best option is to pop into a bar – nobody will complain.

COMMUNICATIONS & NEWS

For long-distance phone calls I suggest you use telephone booths or exchanges. If you can avoid it, don't phone from hotels, since the mark-up is steep. The prefix for Tenerife and province is 922. The prefix for Gran Canaria is 928. You don't need to use it within the island nor for Lanzarote or Fuerteventura. To dial other countries (Canada follows the US system) first dial the international access code 07, then the country code: Australia (61); France (33); Germany (49); Italy (39); Japan (81); Netherlands (31); UK (44); US (1). If using a US credit phone card, dial the company's access number below. Sprint, Tel: 900 99 0013; AT&T, Tel: 900 99 00 11; MCI, Tel: 900 99 0014. Gran Canaria has three newspapers – *Canarias 7*, *La Provincia* and *Diario de Las Palmas*. All major European daily newspapers are on the news stands the day following publication.

USEFUL ADDRESSES

Tourist Information

Spanish National Tourist Office
57–58 St James' Street
London SW1
Tel: (71) 499 4593/499 3257

Oficina de Turismo
Parque Santa Catalina, Las Palmas
Tel: 277356

Consulates

France
Calle Néstor de la Torre, 12
Tel: 244012

Germany
Calle José Franchy y Roca, 5
Tel: 275700

United Kingdom
Calle Luis Morote, 6
Tel: 262508

United States
Calle José Franchy y Roca, 5–5°
Tel: 271259

FURTHER READING

Insight Guide: Gran Canaria, Lanzarote and Fuerteventura is a good background. If you want to walk across and around Gran Canaria, the Sunflower Countryside Guide, *Landscapes of Gran Canaria* by Noel Rochford, provides a sensible and comprehensive selection of tours, some of which form part of the Tourist Board's new project to restore the *caminos reales* (royal routes) which linked towns before the island's roads were developed. For culture vultures, the CAAM (El Centro Atlantico de Arte Moderno) publishes all its catalogues in bi-lingual (English/Spanish) editions.

Sunset over Roque Nublo, with Tenerife's Mt Teide in the distance

Index

A

Agaete 31, 36, 40, 68, 73, 81
Agüimes 43, 57, 72
La Aldea 52
Andamana, Princess 14
antiques 22, 25
Aquasur 58–9
Arguineguin 50, 61
art galleries 23, 24, 44, 45, 46, 79
Arteara 55
Artenara 36, 40, 73
Arucas 32
La Atalaya 34
Atlantic Centre of Modern Art (CAAM) 24, 81
Atlantis 13

B

bananas 17, 29, 43
Bandama 34, 80
banks 76–7, 78
Bañaderos 29, 38, 80
Barranco de Amadores 51
Barranco de Guayadeque 41, 42–3, 57, 66
bars 40, 56, 60, 69, 70
basketry 62
beaches 27, 30, 31, 43, 51, 52, 60, 80
Bentejuí 29
'bienmesabe' 35, 57, 65
boat trips 60, 61
British 17, 19, 29, 34
Brown, Samler 16
buses 74, 77
business hours 78
Bute, Marquis of 44
Los Berrazales 31–2

C

Cabo Verde 38
Los Caideros 51
Caldera de Bandama 34
camel safaris 10–1, 55–6, 58
camping 79
car hire 77
Carnival 43, 69, 72, 81
Casa-Museo de los Manrique (Teror) 36
Casa-Museo de Tomás Morales (Moya) 39
casino 53
caves 29–30, 42, 66
Cenobio de Valerón 14, 29
cheese 29, 33, 64–5
Chirino, Martin 16
Cho Zacarías 35
churches 3, 31, 36–7, 38, 41
CICA 44
climate 74–5
cochineal 17, 19
Columbus, Christopher 16, 19, 24
La Concepción 35
consulates 81
credit cards 77
crime 80
Cruz de Tejeda 35
Cuatro Puertas 14, 42
Cubillo, Antonio 16
Cueva Pintada 29–30
Cuevas de las Cruces 30
cuisine, local 64, 65–6

D, E

Dedo de Díos 31
discos 27, 37, 69, 70, 71
dogs 13, 19, 23
'drago' (dragon tree) 15, 33, 63
Drake, Sir Francis 19, 73
Earthways 40
EC (European Community) 18, 76
electricity 76
embroidery 26, 48
emergencies 80
Ermita de las Nieves 31

F

Ferdinand and Isabella 15, 19, 24
Feria del Atlántico 37
ferries 61, 77
festivals 37, 68, 71–3, 78, 79
fish 64, 66
flowers 48, 63
Fontanales 40
football 80
El Fraile 36, 56
Franco, General 19, 25
Fuerteventura 17, 74, 76, 77, 81
furniture 41

G

Gáldar 14, 29, 41, 73
Gallardo, Tony 16, 28
Gando airport 74, 78
La Garita 43
geography 76
geology 13
go-karting 58
'godos' 18
'gofio' 17, 37, 43, 63, 64
golf 34, 59, 80
Gomera 15
Greeks 12, 19
'guanartemes' 14, 19, 26, 29
Guanches 12, 14, 15, 16, 17, 19, 29, 30, 41, 43, 44, 49
Guía 29
guidebooks 17, 81
Güigüi 52, 53

H

handicrafts 25, 26, 42, 57, 62
'harimaguadas' 14, 42
health 79–80
El Hierro 14, 65
Holidayworld 60
horse-riding 58
hospitals 79, 80
hotels 26, 27, 34, 37, 51, 53, 56, 78–9
Hoya de Pineda 40

I, J, K

'ídolos de Tara' 41, 43, 63
Ingenio 42, 73
La Isleta 73
Jardín Canario 33
Juba II 13, 19
'juego del garrote' 14, 80
Kraus, Alfredo 25

L

language 15
Lanzarote 27, 63, 66, 74, 76, 81
Las Lagunas 56
Las Palmas 13, 17, 18, 19, 20, 21–7, 43, 44, 46–8, 74, 75, 77, 78, 79, 81
  Avenida Marítima 26, 77
  Biblioteca Insular 44
  British Club 26
  Cabildo 45
  Calle de los Balcones 24
  Calle Ripoche 47, 80
  Las Canteras 46, 63, 77, 78
  Las Canteras beach 27, 80
  Casa de Colón 22–3
  Casa-Museo Benito Pérez Galdós 45
  Catedral Santa Ana 23–4
  Centro Insular de Cultura 45
  Gabinete Literario 25
  Mesa y López 46, 62, 63
  Museo Canario 15, 43–4
  Museum of Religious Art 23
  Parque Santa Catalina 17, 27, 46, 62, 81
  Paseo de las Canteras 27
  Plaza de la Victoria 69–70
  Plaza de las Ranas 44
  Plaza Santa Ana 23
  Plaza Santo Domingo 44
  Pueblo Canario 26, 62
  Puente de Piedra 22
  La Regenta 46
  San Antonio Abad 24–5
  Teatro Guiniguada 22
  Teatro Pérez Galdós 21, 79
  Town Hall 23

Triana 22, 25, 46, 47, 63, 69
Vegueta 22, 44, 62, 69, 73, 77
Leacock buildings 29
'lucha canaria' 14, 57, 71, 80

M

El Madroñal 35
maps 81
markets 22, 35, 37
Maspalomas 53, 59, 60, 70, 72, 75, 79, 80
Massieu, Padorno and Lola 16
Melenara 43
Las Meloneras 53
Millares family 16
Miller and Elder 17
Mogán 52, 57, 61, 73, 79
'mojo' sauce 25, 35, 65
Montaña Arena 49
Montaña Vergara 40
El Montañón 57
Moya 38–9
mummies 14, 15, 43
Museo de Piedras 42, 73
museums 22, 23, 35, 36, 39, 42, 43–4, 45, 57, 73
music 63, 73, 79
musical intruments 26, 62
mythology 12, 13

N, O

'naife' 15, 26, 62
newspapers 81
nightlife 68–70
nudism 60
Ocean Park 60
ONCE 46

P

Los Palmitos Park 58
Panchito 34
parador 36, 56
Pasito Blanco 49, 60, 79
passports 75
'pastelerías' 35, 45
Patalavaca 51, 60, 79
Los Pechos 56
'Pendón de la Conquista' 24
Pérez Galdós, Benito 19, 21, 45
Phoenicians 19
Pinar de Inagua 57
Pinar de Tamadaba 32, 36, 40
'pintaderas' 16, 30, 43, 62, 63
Playa del Hombre 43
Playa del Inglés 53, 60, 74, 75, 79
Pliny 13, 19
police 80
politics 16, 76
population 19, 76, 77
Portuguese 17, 19, 42
potatoes 17, 25, 65
pottery 34, 48, 62
Power, Teobaldo 63
Pozo Izquierdo 80
Presa de Chira 56
public holidays *see* festivals
Puente de Silva 29
Puerto de la Luz 73
Puerto de las Nieves 6–7, 31
Puerto de Mogán 57
Puerto Rico 51, 52, 61, 75, 80

R

El Rancho Verde 58
Real de Las Palmas 19
religion 14, 76
Reptilandia 30
restaurants 25, 26, 27, 30, 31, 32, 33, 35, 36, 37, 40, 42, 48, 51, 52, 53, 55, 56, 57, 59, 60, 65–7
El Rincón 28
Romans 12, 13, 19
Roque Bentaiga 36, 40, 57
Roque Nublo 36, 40, 56
rum 26, 27

S

sailing 60
San Agustín 53, 79, 80
San Bartolomé de Tirajana 73
San Borondón 76
San Gregorio 73
San Mateo 35, 40
San Nicolás de Tolentino 52, 73
Sanabria, Falcón 63
'sancocho' 43, 64
Santa Brígida 35, 40
Santa Lucía 57
El Sao 32
Sardina del Norte 30
shark-fishing 61, 80
shops 22, 24, 25, 26, 44–5, 46–8, 57, 60, 62–3, 78
slaves 17, 42

souvenirs 46, 62–3
Spanish Civil War 19
Spanish invasion 12, 14, 15, 19, 44
sports 80
Suaréz, Adolfo 16
sugar 17, 19, 42

T

Tafira 34
Tafira Baja 33
Taidía 57
Taurito 51–2, 75, 79
taxis 74, 77, 78
Teide, Mt (Tenerife) 27, 36, 40, 56, 81
Tejeda 56
Telde 41–2, 73
telephones 81
Tenerife 18, 27, 36, 40, 43, 52, 56, 74, 76, 77, 80
Tenesor Semidan 19
Teror 36–7, 67, 73
time differences 76
tipping 77
Tirma, Mt 14
Los Tiros de Moya 39
tobacco 63
tomatoes 16, 25, 43
de la Torre, Manuel Martin Fernández 26
de la Torre, Néstor 26
tourism 18, 19
tourist information offices 78, 81
Túmulo de la Guancha 30
Tunte 54, 56
'turrón' 37, 63, 65

V

El Valle 31
Valleseco 36
Van der Hoes 19, 35
Vecindario 43, 57
'vela latina' 80
Veneguera 52
Vera, Pedro de 19
Virgen de la Cuevita 40
Virgen del Pino 37

W, Z

water 80
water sports 51, 60, 61, 80
wine 16, 19, 27, 35, 63, 65
zoo 52

Art & Photo Credits

Cover **Rick Strange**
Photography **Paul Young** *and*
Pages 12, 13, 14, 15, 16T, 34T, 47T, 74 **Andrew Eames**
5B, 26, 33, 80 **Wolfgang Fritz**
25, 66T, 72 **Tulio Gatti**
35, 53T, 64, 67B, 68, 75B, 76, 77B, 78 **Roger Hilton**
27B, 66 **Sergio Rodriguez Matos**
59T, 63B, 65, 79 **Nigel Tisdall**
71 **Bill Wassman**

Handwriting **V. Barl**
Production Editor **Erich Meyer**
Cover Design **Klaus Geisler**
Cartography **Berndtson & Berndtson**

INSIGHT GUIDES

COLORSET NUMBERS

160 Alaska
155 Alsace
150 Amazon Wildlife
116 America, South
173 American Southwest
158A Amsterdam
260 Argentina
287 Asia, East
207 Asia, South
262 Asia, South East
194 Asian Wildlife, Southeast
167A Athens
272 Australia
263 Austria
188 Bahamas
206 Bali Baru
107 Baltic States
246A Bangkok
292 Barbados
219B Barcelona
187 Bay of Naples
234A Beijing
109 Belgium
135A Berlin
217 Bermuda
100A Boston
127 Brazil
178 Brittany
109A Brussels
144A Budapest
260A Buenos Aires
213 Burgundy
268A Cairo
247B Calcutta
275 California
180 California, Northern
161 California, Southern
237 Canada
162 Caribbean The Lesser Antilles
122 Catalonia (Costa Brava)
141 Channel Islands
184C Chicago
151 Chile
234 China
135E Cologne
119 Continental Europe
189 Corsica
281 Costa Rica
291 Cote d'Azur
165 Crete
184 Crossing America
226 Cyprus
114 Czechoslovakia
247A Delhi, Jaipur, Agra
238 Denmark
135B Dresden
142B Dublin
135F Düsseldorf

204 East African Wildlife
149 Eastern Europe,
118 Ecuador
148A Edinburgh
268 Egypt
123 Finland
209B Florence
243 Florida
154 France
135C Frankfurt
208 Gambia & Senegal
135 Germany
148B Glasgow
279 Gran Canaria
169 Great Barrier Reef
124 Great Britain
167 Greece
166 Greek Islands
135G Hamburg
240 Hawaii
193 Himalaya, Western
196 Hong Kong
144 Hungary
256 Iceland
247 India
212 India, South
128 Indian Wildlife
143 Indonesia
142 Ireland
252 Israel
236A Istanbul
209 Italy
213 Jamaica
278 Japan
266 Java
252A Jerusalem-Tel Aviv
203A Kathmandu
270 Kenya
300 Korea
202A Lisbon
258 Loire Valley
124A London
275A Los Angeles
201 Madeira
219A Madrid
145 Malaysia
157 Mallorca & Ibiza
117 Malta
272B Melbourne
285 Mexico
285A Mexico City
243A Miami
237B Montreal
235 Morocco
101A Moscow
135D Munich
211 Myanmar (Burma)
259 Namibia
269 Native America
203 Nepal
158 Netherlands

100 New England
184E New Orleans
184F New York City
133 New York State
293 New Zealand
265 Nile, The
120 Norway
124B Oxford
147 Pacific Northwest
205 Pakistan
154A Paris
249 Peru
184B Philadelphia
222 Philippines
115 Poland
202 Portugal
114A Prague
153 Provence
156 Puerto Rico
250 Rajasthan
177 Rhine
127A Rio de Janeiro
172 Rockies
209A Rome
101 Russia
275B San Francisco
130 Sardinia
148 Scotland
184D Seattle
261 Sicily
159 Singapore
257 South Africa
264 South Tyrol
219 Spain
220 Spain, Southern
105 Sri Lanka
101B St Petersburg
170 Sweden
232 Switzerland
272 Sydney
175 Taiwan
112 Tenerife
186 Texas
246 Thailand
278A Tokyo
139 Trinidad & Tobago
113 Tunisia
236 Turkey
171 Turkish Coast
210 Tuscany
174 Umbria
237A Vancouver
198 Venezuela
209C Venice
263A Vienna
255 Vietnam
267 Wales
184C Washington DC
183 Waterways of Europe
215 Yemen

You'll find the colorset number on the spine of each Insight Guide.

INSIGHT *POCKET* GUIDES

EXISTING & FORTHCOMING TITLES:

Aegean Islands
Algarve
Alsace
Athens
Bali
Bali Bird Walks
Bangkok
Barcelona
Bavaria
Berlin
Bhutan
Boston
Brittany
Brussels
Budapest & *Surroundings*
Canton
Chiang Mai
Costa Blanca
Costa Brava
Cote d'Azur
Crete
Denmark
Florence
Florida
Gran Canaria
Hawaii
Hong Kong
Ibiza
Ireland
Istanbul
Jakarta
Kathmandu *Bikes & Hikes*
Kenya
Kuala Lumpur
Lisbon
Loire Valley
London
Macau
Madrid
Malacca
Mallorca
Malta
Marbella/ *Costa del Sol*
Miami
Milan
Morocco
Moscow
Munich
Nepal
New Delhi
New York City
North California
Oslo/Bergen
Paris
Penang
Phuket
Prague
Provence
Rhodes
Rome
Sabah
San Francisco
Sardinia
Scotland
Seville/Grenada
Seychelles
Sikkim
Singapore
South California
Southeast England
Sri Lanka
St Petersburg
Sydney
Tenerife
Thailand
Tibet
Turkish Coast
Tuscany
Venice
Vienna
Yogyakarta
Yugoslavia's *Adriatic Coast*

United States: **Houghton Mifflin Company, Boston MA 02108**
Tel: (800) 2253362 Fax: (800) 4589501

Canada: **Thomas Allen & Son, 390 Steelcase Road East**
Markham, Ontario L3R 1G2
Tel: (416) 4759126 Fax: (416) 4756747

Great Britain: **GeoCenter UK, Hampshire RG22 4BJ**
Tel: (256) 817987 Fax: (256) 817988

Worldwide: **Höfer Communications Singapore 2262**
Tel: (65) 8612755 Fax: (65) 8616438

"I was first drawn to the Insight Guides by the excellent "Nepal" volume. I can think of no book which so effectively captures the essence of a country. Out of these pages leaped the Nepal I know – the captivating charm of a people and their culture. I've since discovered and enjoyed the entire Insight Guide Series. Each volume deals with a country or city in the same sensitive depth, which is nowhere more evident than in the superb photography."

Sir Edmund Hillary

NOTES